MIND-
BOGGLING
BUILDINGS

MIND-BOGGLING BUILDINGS

— MICHAEL COX —

Illustrated by
Mike Phillips

Hippo

Scholastic Children's Books,
Commonwealth House, 1–19 New Oxford Street,
London WC1A 1NU, UK

A division of Scholastic Limited
London ~ New York ~ Toronto ~ Sydney ~ Auckland
Mexico City ~ New Delhi ~ Hong Kong

Published in the UK by Scholastic Ltd, 1998

ISBN 0 590 19863 7

Typeset by TW Typesetting, Midsomer Norton, Somerset
Printed and bound in Great Britain by The Bath Press, Bath

2 4 6 8 10 9 7 5 3

Contents

Michael Cox single-handedly designed and built what was thought to be one of the most stylish fortified buildings of its day. Unfortunately, 20 minutes later, the tide came in and washed his sandcastle away. These days he is particularly interested in the multi-storey constructions which are found in city centres everywhere and says he often spends whole weekends wandering around them trying to remember where he parked his car.

Mike Phillips enjoys illustrating amazing, eye-catching buildings. He also enjoys lazing about watching TV in them, eating vast quantities of food in them and having a lie-in on Sundays in them. Once, he built, with his own two hands, a dazzling skyscraper of such beauty it brought a tear to the eye, until the dog knocked it over and ate one of the Lego pieces. He currently lives in Essex and the dog lives in the garden.

INTRODUCTION

Have you ever been on holiday and come face to face with one of those buildings that are just so breathtakingly beautiful that people from all over the world come to see them in their thousands?

You know the sort of buildings don't you – the ones that are either so old, or so huge, or so incredibly original in their form and structure ... that they are nothing short of mind-boggling! Lots of people know about these mind-boggling buildings because they've seen them on the telly, or on souvenir T-shirts and tea towels. They know that they're *very*, *very* remarkable – but quite often, that's about as far as it goes...

Would you like to find out more about mind-boggling buildings? For instance, have you ever wondered:

- How they all came to be there in the first place?
- Who thought them up?
- How they were built?
- What they were for and …
- How they came to look the way they do?

You couldn't possibly visit all of the mind-boggling buildings in the world – there are just too many of them, it would cost you a fortune in airline tickets and more to the point, it would make you late for school. So read this book instead! You can jet off on a mind-boggling building safari of your own *and* have tonnes of fun along the way – all without leaving the security of your favourite armchair, school cell or comfy straitjacket.

Hopefully, you'll return from your trip bursting with so many fascinating facts about famous (and not-quite-so-famous) buildings that your friends will gibber with admiration and your teacher will whimper with envy!

Want to know…

Who got 15,000 builders to come round to his house and do a few alterations … because he was shy!

How the builders of the Eiffel Tower got really attached to their work?

Which royal palace had 1,300 rooms, 20,000 occupants … but no loos?

Plus a whole lot more – read on!

SUPERSTAR STRUCTURES

There are masses of mind-boggling buildings all over the world, but *some* buildings are even more mind-boggling than others! They're the mind-boggling building "superstars" and are sometimes described as "wonders of the world" because they're such perfect examples of everything that was daring, exciting, imaginative and forward thinking about architecture and building at the time they were built. Many of these architectural "one and onlys" have been around for so long that some people just can't imagine what the world would be like without them.

PARIS WOULDN'T BE PARIS WITHOUT THE EIFFEL TOWER

WHAT WOULD IT BE?

TOKYO?

Tourists taking a stroll around Paris before 1887 would have had *no* problems visualizing the city without the Eiffel Tower, because it didn't exist. The mind-boggling structure that was destined to become such a world-famous landmark was still taking shape inside the imagination of its brilliant creator ... Gustave Eiffel!

This is how Gustave's amazing idea became reality...

Ooh – you are *Eiffel* ... but we like you!

Towards the end of the 19th century the French people were planning to celebrate the 100th anniversary of the revolution in which they'd overthrown their awful upper classes. Their intention was to hold a huge exhibition of their achievements on the banks of the River Seine in Paris to show just how far they'd come since getting rid of the enemy. They needed a really spectacular archway entrance for the whole thing so they organized a competition to see who could come up with the best design. The engineer, Gustave Eiffel (1832–1923), designed a tall tower which the organizers thought stood head and shoulders above the opposition – he won the competition, construction

IT'S AN **EIFFEL** LONG WAY UP...

10

work began in 1887 and the Eiffel Tower became the wonder of its day!

Some Eiffely fascinating facts about the tower

1 The Eiffel Tower is constructed from lots of separate pieces – just like a model kit – but instead of having just a hundred or so plastic bits, it had *18,038* metal parts that weighed approximately *6,400 tonnes*.

2 The components (parts) for the tower's lattice (criss-cross) framework were made from wrought iron – that's the very strong metal that ornamental gates are sometimes made from. This sort of metal is difficult to weld (heat to form a join) so the separate components had to be connected by rivets, which were heated before they were hammered into place.

...AND AN **EIFFEL** LONG WAY DOWN!

3 Lots of care had to be taken in the manufacture of the components – if any of the holes for the *two-and-a-half million* rivets didn't match perfectly it would be impossible to make a successful join. The location of every single rivet hole had to be shown on the *5,000* different diagrams, which were drawn by a team of engineers.

4 The parts were pre-fabricated (ready-made) at a separate workshop, one-and-a-half kilometres from the building site. They were then brought to the site from the workshop on horse-drawn carts.

5 The tower was a maths teacher's dream. Its unusual form was created from hundreds of really varied and complex shapes and angles. Absolutely nothing could be left to chance – so thousands of calculations had to be made in order to get each bit of the structure to slot perfectly into place.

6 As the workers struggled to erect the steel frame on cold winter days their hands became frozen to the metal – just as your tongue or lips can get frozen to ice lollies. When they tried to free them, great chunks of their skin were torn off and left sticking to the tower!

So ... what do you think of it then?

When the tower was put up, many people had very strong feelings about it. For example, the famous French author, Guy de Maupassant (1850–93), liked nothing better than to have his meals in one of the restaurants that were built inside it. Why?

a) They served the tastiest pommes frites (French chips) in town.

b) He thought the tower was the nearest thing to paradise on Earth.

c) It was the only place in Paris that he couldn't actually see the Eiffel Tower from.

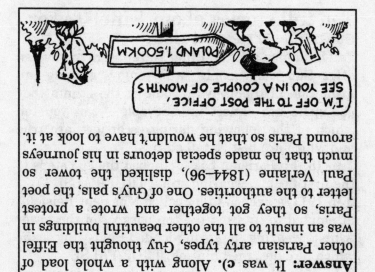

Answer: It was c). Along with a whole load of other Parisian arty types, Guy thought the Eiffel was an insult to all the other beautiful buildings in Paris, so they got together and wrote a protest letter to the authorities. One of Guy's pals, the poet Paul Verlaine (1844–96), disliked the tower so much that he made special detours in his journeys around Paris so that he wouldn't have to look at it.

As everyone now knows the mathematician was wrong – the tower was finished in May 1889 in time for the Paris Exhibition and it's managed to stay standing ever since ... all thanks to Gustave's engineering skills.

Ten tall stories about Eiffel Tower stunts – true or false?

Tall buildings like the Eiffel Tower seem to have an attraction for people who enjoy making an exhibition of themselves. Some of the stunts they get up to are almost unbelievable – can you tell which of the following daring escapades are true and which are just ... tall stories?

1 In 1891 a Parisian baker climbed the 363 steps to the first floor ... wearing stilts! TRUE/FALSE

2 In 1911, a French tailor called Monsieur Reisfeldt attempted to fly from the top parapet of the tower whilst wearing a spring-loaded, bat-wing cape which he'd designed himself. TRUE/FALSE

3 In 1905 the world's first-ever bungee jump was

made from the tower by French acrobat, Pierre Letissier. After attaching himself to an elasticated rope and leaping from the top platform he immediately catapulted back up ... then dropped down again! TRUE/FALSE

4 In June 1923 a French sports writer called Pierre Labric rode a bicycle down the steps from the top of the first floor to the bottom of the ground floor. TRUE/FALSE

5 In November 1926 – in an attempt to impress his brother who lived near by – a 23-year-old Frenchman called Leon Collot tried to fly an aeroplane through the gap between the tower's legs. TRUE/FALSE

6 During the Second World War – just a few days after the Allied Forces had successfully recaptured Paris from the Germans – an American pilot attempted a similar flying stunt. TRUE/FALSE

7 In 1964 a group of mountaineers climbed the tower – and they didn't use the stairs! TRUE/FALSE

8 In 1968 a cow was hoisted up the tower to encourage people to buy dairy products like milk, butter and cheese. TRUE/FALSE

9 In 1967 a top Paris chef hoisted a large rabbit from the ground to the top of the tower in an attempt to publicize the opening of his new restaurant, "Le Lapin Aeronautique" (The Flying Rabbit). TRUE/FALSE

10 Every year the tower itself performs a rather amazing stunt of its own – it grows taller! TRUE/FALSE

Answers:

1 True

2 True – unfortunately, Monsieur Reisfeldt's home-made "caped crusader" outfit failed to keep him airborne and he plunged to his death in front of a huge crowd. He hit the ground with such force that he made a hole nearly 30 cm (12 in) deep. Doctors who examined his body afterwards thought he'd probably died of a heart attack before he'd hit the ground.

3 False

4 True

5 True – Leon was almost successful, but at the last moment he was temporarily blinded by the rays of the rising sun. This caused him to veer to the left and collide with an antenna cable. The plane immediately burst into flames and he was killed.

6 True – this time the attempt was successful. The American pilot managed to fly his aeroplane between the tower's legs without mishap (he must have been wearing his sunglasses).

7 True – the tower was scaled by the mountaineers as part of the celebrations for its 75th birthday.

8 True

9 False

10 True – on hot summer days the tower has a growth spurt and becomes up to 17 cm (7 in) higher as heat causes its metal components to expand – as they cool off it shrinks back to its normal size.

Another world-famous monument that Gustave helped build was the enormous metal woman known as the Statue of Liberty.

Despite being America's best-known landmark, Liberty originally came from France – so sooner or later she would have needed to make some sort of application for formal acceptance into her new country...

UNITED STATES OF AMERICA APPLICATION FOR US CITIZENSHIP AND PASSPORT

Please answer all questions

Name Statue of Liberty.

Address Liberty Island, New York Harbour, USA.

Claim to fame The best-known landmark in America.

Vital statistics
Height: 93 m (305 ft)
Waist: 11 m (35 ft)
Right arm: 13 m (42ft)

Nose: 1 metre (3 ft)
Eyes: 0.8 m (2½ ft)
Face: 3 m (9.8 ft) wide ...

Colour of skin Originally copper ... now green, due to standing around in perishing damp for over 100 years.

Distinguishing features Well yes I've ... ermm ... err ... got a *door* in the sole of my right foot. We've all got our little peculiarities you know!

Notable *internal* features Top to toe spiral staircase – which the tourists use to get to the

viewing platform inside my head (bloomin' *liberty* if you ask me!).

Country of origin France.

Reason for coming to America Gift from the French people to the Americans to celebrate the 100th anniversary of their independence from Britain.

Method of travel to America I was assembled in France ... *then* taken to pieces again ... *then* packed into 210 wooden cases ... *then* shipped across the Atlantic ... *then* finally reassembled! It's not easy being a national monument, you know!

Creators' occupations Builders, sculptors, engineers.

Main creators' names

Gustave Eiffel He did my internal skeleton – that's the 1,700 bar framework that supports the 300 copper plates of my "skin", it's about the thickness of a small coin. I think my skeleton may have been a sort of practice for Gustave's tower.

Frederic Bartholdi Sculpted me by making lots of clay models to start with. The sheets of copper were laid over wooden "moulds" based on the models then beaten by metal workers. It took  thousands of detailed measurements to get me right. In fact, the whole job took them 21 years … but I think you'll agree I'm well worth it!

Take after anyone? Mrs Bartholdi – that's Fred's mum. He modelled my face on her. He based the rest of me on some ancient Roman sculptures!

Any "living" relatives Smaller identical sister on the banks of the River Seine in Paris.

Hand luggage *Left hand* – Enormous tablet made from stone with the date of American independence –

4 July 1776 – chiselled into it.
Right hand – Flaming great torch.

Headwear Crown with seven rays each representing freedom spreading across seven oceans to seven continents.

Occupation Holding up the "light of truth" (flaming torch!). Standing for the human "ideals" of truth, liberty and equality, and being a welcoming beacon to boatloads of new immigrants and visitors arriving in the USA.

Secondary occupation Symbolizing the great 19th-century progress in building and engineering technology that enabled me to be created in the first place.

Physical complaints Yes, my right arm's killing me – this torch weighs a tonne!

Gustave Eiffel learned an awful lot about new materials and construction methods by working on lots of other jobs – like the Statue of Liberty and various bridge building projects – before he got the know-how to build his amazing tower. It's never been different – builders, architects and engineers have always had to come up with new materials and techniques to turn their dreams into mind-boggling reality.

Ancient Roman archi'facts

A well-known architect once said that "the basic nature of architecture is its holes". One of the big problems that faced the builders of long ago was how to make "holes" or openings in a structure – so that they could get in and out – without actually weakening the whole thing so much that it fell down.

If an ancient builder wanted to put a door or window into a wall, they had to support it with a stone or wooden beam known as a **lintel** to stop the bit of wall above it falling down. If the gap was a *really big* gap, a *really big* lintel had to be used – and this meant a *really big* struggle, because most builders didn't have arms like mountain gorillas, or modern mechanical building aids like bulldozers and cranes to help them.

Instead of enormous lintels, Roman builders began to use **arches**. The ancient Egyptians and Greeks had actually used these incredibly useful and attractive forms before them, but the Romans were the first people to get really ambitious – and as they developed more and more versatile and effective arches they were able to construct bigger and better buildings!

Some Roman archi'techniques

They made really big arches called **viaducts** which held roads up over valleys and waterways – which look like this...

...and **aqueducts** which were used to carry water, which look like this...

They made extended arches that were called **vaults**...

They made semi-circular vaults called **barrel vaults** that looked like this...

And they joined several **barrel vaults** up to make a **cross vault** that looked like this...

If arches are so strong and look so good you may be wondering why your local superstore isn't full of them. Well, nowadays, builders are able to bridge wide gaps with lintels made from steel or reinforced concrete and also have much better ways of putting them in place.

Some concrete Roman building facts

The ancient Egyptians and Greeks built many of their great buildings with stone. Stone is hard to work with – it has to be chiselled into shape before it will fit the gap you want to fill. A much easier solution is to have a liquid building material that will slip into a space, then set as hard as stone.

The clever Romans invented a really strong sort of "liquid rock" with this recipe...

What you need:
volcanic rock (called pozzolana)
burnt limestone
sand
stones
water

What to do:
Mix all ingredients thoroughly and pour into the shape or mould you wish to fill. Allow to set – keep away from dogs and children who might want to stick their paws in and leave prints.

We use a version of this mind-boggling mixture today ... it's called concrete. One of the buildings the Romans created using concrete was the Colosseum where gory battles took place (so an awful lot of people and animals would have been very happy if concrete had never been invented)...

THE COLOSSEUM
BUILT between AD 72 and AD 80

UNDERGROUND - Cells and corridors for keeping wild animals and gladiators, formed from VAULTED ARCHES and BARREL VAULTS

NUMBERED ENTRANCES - 76 of these - tickets have entrance and seat numbers on so people can get in and out quickly

GATE OF DEATH - the dead and dying are whipped away through this

WHY DO US POOR FOLK HAVE TO SIT RIGHT AT THE TOP, MUM?

'COS THERE'LL BE FURTHER TO FALL IF THE STADIUM COLLAPSES!

VELARIUM – a canvas cover attached to 240 poles to make an all-weather stadium

TIERED SEATS – the poorer you are the higher up you have to sit

LIFTS – raise contestants and animals from underground cells

FOUL! OFFSIDE!

I THINK YOU'RE AT THE WRONG STADIUM

VAULTED ARCHES – make the whole place strong enough to hold the weight of 50,000 people

ARENA – Slaughter spectaculars take place here, sometimes so many animals are killed that in some parts of the empire whole species are wiped out
(ARENA IS LATIN FOR SAND)

27

The Colosseum was built on the site of a drained lake. Sometimes the arena was filled with water supplied from an **aqueduct** so great sea battles could be re-enacted for the entertainment of the audience. The Emperor Tiberius once organized a mega-spectacular event involving 100 ships and 19,000 men.

All that remains of the Colosseum today are the enormous ruins that stand in the centre of Rome. Tourists wishing to see people writhing in agony and making horrible blood-curdling noises should go to an Italian pop concert.

IT'S JUST NOT THE SAME WITHOUT THE BLOOD

WAIL

Mind-boggling fact
If the Romans got fed up with seeing gladiators and wild animals being torn to shreds at the Colosseum, they may well have popped along to the Circus Maximus to enjoy some Formula One chariot racing. The Circus Maximus is no longer standing. In fact, a whole section of its tiered seating collapsed, killing over 1,000 spectators, during the second century AD (had they all been jumping up and down with excitement?) ... and in the fourth century AD "rubble makers", known as the Vandals and the Goths, may have had something to do with its destruction.

Watch out ... here come the rubble makers!

After ruling the roost for centuries the Roman Empire began to crumble, but many of its buildings didn't – they were too well-built! Invading tribes – such as the Vandals and the Goths – who came sweeping down from northern Europe armed to the teeth with swords and axes had a really good go at turning 800 years of Roman architectural achievement into nothing more than a huge heap of crazy paving material but, despite their efforts, almost 2,000 years later many of the great buildings of the Roman Empire are still standing.

Going ... going ... con!

Every year thousands of tourists pay large amounts of money to see superstar structures like the Eiffel Tower, the Statue of Liberty and the Colosseum, and this makes big profits for the people who own or run the sites. In one way or another, owning buildings often makes people rich – especially if they sell them for a lot more than they paid for them. Just imagine what it would be like to own some of the world's most mind-boggling buildings and then be able to sell them whenever you were in need of the odd bit of pocket money. Arthur Furguson, a retired actor, didn't *imagine* that he owned the great buildings of the world ... he actually *pretended* that he did ... then "sold" them to anyone who was daft enough to buy them. Believe it or not, there were plenty of idiots willing to cough up the readies! This is what happened.

30

Arthur got out of jail in 1930 – he didn't manage to sell *that* – but he did manage to live a life of luxury in Los Angeles (paid for by more confidence tricks) until he died in 1938.

PSST!...WANNA BUY A GRAVEYARD?

One mind-boggling building that Arthur might have had a bit of trouble finding a buyer for is the Great Wall of China. The wall was built in the first century AD by Quin Shihuang Di, the first emperor of China.

A bit of writing on the wall
The Great Wall of China is the largest structure in the world and is said to be the only man-made object on Earth that can be seen from outer space.

There had been other walls on the Chinese border before Quin took over, but they weren't joined up. Ferocious Mongolian tribesmen from the north were forever nipping through the gaps and causing trouble...

YOU AGAIN?

Quin didn't actually build the wall on his own – he had a bit of help from 30,000 labourers. Quin and the labourers had a special arrangement – he got all the big ideas and they got all the big blisters and backaches. The wall is sometimes called the Wall of Tears or The World's Longest Graveyard because so many of the labourers died during its construction – many of them are said to be buried inside it.

Quin was very fussy about quality control – he said that if a workman left a gap between the stones that was large enough to fit a nail into he should be hanged on the spot.

Eight steps to keep out the riff-raff

1 *Plan* the route of your wall along the northern border of your empire – it will climb great mountain ranges, cross hostile deserts and straddle stinking swamps – and will eventually be about 5,000 miles long (give or take a few twists and turns). Don't forget to set up supply camps and build roads for transporting workers, food and materials.

2 Build 25,000 watchtowers all along the planned route of the wall so that the workers can be

protected from the ferocious tribes who don't think it's a very good idea in the first place.

3 Construct the watchtowers at intervals of about two arrow shots apart – so that archers can pick off any troublemakers.

4 Dig foundations for the main wall between the watchtowers. Warning – sometimes it will be very windy. After you have dug the same foundation trench 16 or 17 times, only to see the soil blown straight back into it, you may begin to get a bit fed up – so build a windbreak first … a little wall would be just the thing!

5 Build the central section of the main wall from soil and rubble, giving it an outer surface of stone or bricks and mortar.

6 Cover the top of your wall with bricks, slabs or

stone. Make the top of the wall wide enough for ten foot-soldiers to walk along it. When urgent help is needed, troops of cavalry will be able to gallop along it five abreast and reach trouble spots really quickly.

7 Build a 2 m (7 ft) high parapet along the north-facing side of your wall. Leave narrow gaps in it so that your soldiers can shoot arrows and lob boulders at the Mongol attackers. Build another parapet on the south-facing side of your wall.

8 Instruct the garrisons of soldiers who guard the wall to keep in touch with each other by a series of beacon fires. Devise a system of coded warnings. For example: for a medium-sized emergency – about 500 enemy warriors approaching the wall! – send up a single column of smoke or flame.

THEY'VE BURNT THE CHIPS AGAIN!

For a really big emergency – say, an army of 10,000 heavily armed enemies (all with huge moustaches and horrible haircuts!) is on its way to invade China – send up four columns of smoke.

Last brick

Today, some parts of the Great Wall of China get so busy with tourists that enormous human traffic jams build up. It's the same at many of the world's superstar structures. Great buildings are so fascinating that people will queue for ages – often after having travelled halfway round the world – just to experience the thrill of their special atmosphere first hand.

HEAVEN ON EARTH

Lots of mind-boggling buildings are constructed because people have felt an overwhelming urge to create a little bit of "heaven on Earth" for their chosen gods. As you'd expect, the people who construct these buildings think their gods are the tops, so they put in an enormous effort to make the buildings particularly magnificent.

Two-and-half thousand years ago the ancient Greeks built one of the most famous and magnificent heavenly homes ever seen on Earth.

The Parthenon – the temple that's top of the Acropolis

During the early part of the fifth century BC, the Greek city-state of Athens was at war with Persia (now called Iran). During a particularly bad-tempered home fixture, the Persian army attacked all of the temples that stood on the sacred hill in

Athens, known as the Acropolis. The Athenians were shattered (so were their temples) but they were determined to have their revenge. In 449 BC, they got together with some other Greek city-states and trashed the Persians once and for all. They were so pleased with the victory that they decided to build a really smart new temple called the Parthenon as a tribute to Athena, their goddess of war and wisdom. It was their way of saying ... "Thanks Athena ... we knew you wouldn't let us down!" and, "Look everyone, us Athenians are on top again!"

The Parthenon – building notes

1 Constructed between 447 and 432 BC out of the very hard rock known as marble.

2 Older style Greek temples were quite small and built entirely from wood, or mud and wood.

3 The marble was quarried from Mount Pentelicus – six kilometres (4.5 miles) away from the Acropolis.

4 It was transported to the hill on ox carts. Some marble blocks were so enormous that they were given their own wheels and pulled by up to 30 oxen.

5 Craftsmen cut the marble into shape.
6 Slaves hauled it into place.

We want it to look perfect ... so we'll build on a tilt!

The Parthenon was built at the very top of the Acropolis so that it was always visible to the people in the market place below. The clever ancient Greek architects realized that if the temple was built with regular proportions, it would actually look like this to human eyes viewing it from lower down the hill...

People going about their business in the city below would look up and see it like this and, instead of being awed by the great building, they would just have a good giggle.

So the architect, Iktinos, and the builder, Phidias, had to build it like this...

39

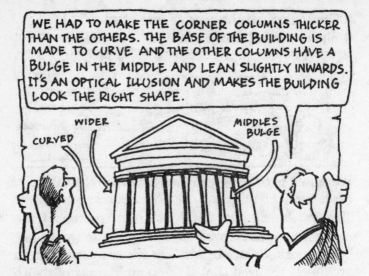

WE HAD TO MAKE THE CORNER COLUMNS THICKER THAN THE OTHERS. THE BASE OF THE BUILDING IS MADE TO CURVE AND THE OTHER COLUMNS HAVE A BULGE IN THE MIDDLE AND LEAN SLIGHTLY INWARDS. IT'S AN OPTICAL ILLUSION AND MAKES THE BUILDING LOOK THE RIGHT SHAPE.

CURVED
WIDER
MIDDLES BULGE

It's all incredibly simple, isn't it?

A column about ... columns!

The Parthenon is surrounded by colonnades – rows of columns. The ancient Greeks were among the first people to use these sturdy but attractive supports for buildings and they've been a hit with architects ever since. This is how this great Greek architectural idea grew up...

1 Early Greek temples (and houses) were built from baked mud. So that sudden showers wouldn't turn them back into heaps of sludge, they were built with overhanging wooden roofs. The roofs were supported by tree trunks.

2 The Greeks liked the look of the tree-trunk supports – so they began to add more and sometimes extended them all the way round their buildings!

3 When the Greeks began building in rock they

40

decided to keep their tree-trunk support idea but, instead of using tree trunks, they made the supports from stone or marble. So the columns are a stone version of the tree trunks.

4 The ancient Greeks became very particular about the way their temples looked. They began decorating the stone columns. They devised elaborate decorations for the capitals (tops). These designs became known as the classical "orders" – because they were part of a set of architectural "rules" that were intended to be followed quite strictly.

Here are the "orders" – they were all used in the Parthenon building...

DORIC   IONIC   CORINTHIAN

It's an absolute classic

In 1889, the famous *Baedeker* travel guide said that the Parthenon was...

The most perfect monument of ancient art and even in ruins is an imposing and soul stirring object.

PARTHENON

The Greek architects were as much artists as they were building designers and wanted to create buildings that were pleasing to the eye and cheering

41

to the spirit. They insisted on precise rules about form and proportions.

The ancient Greek style of building and the Roman style that followed it (and borrowed ideas from it) have since become known as the Classical style of architecture. This Classical style of building has had a really big influence on lots of architecture in Europe and America for the last 2,000 years or so and – right up until the beginning of the 20th century – it was one of the most popular styles around.

Architecture spotting!

If you keep your eyes skinned when you're out and about you'll probably see quite a few buildings that are built in the Classical style, or at least have some Classical features in their design. For example, if your local town hall was built before the 20th century it may well have a colonnade like that of the Parthenon.

The British Museum in London is an excellent example of what is known as Greek Revival architecture.

Its stonking great *façade* (or front bit, as top architects call it) is the spitting image of the entrance to a Greek temple – it could almost be a bit of the Parthenon! Don't be fooled though, this is just a copy – but they have got part of the real thing inside.

Architectural appeal

Sometimes you may see Classical Greek type columns used to give a rather grand look to new houses on modern housing estates, but some people think this looks rather odd.

I NEED TO BE A BASKETBALL PLAYER NOT A POSTMAN!

If you happen to live in a house that looks like this please do not be offended and certainly don't attempt to leave home – it's not *your* fault that your parents have no sense of style – just plant some really fast-growing shrubs at the base of the columns when they're away for the weekend.

Pinnacles of achievement

The Greek word *cathedra* means "throne of god". During the Middle Ages, people in Europe began constructing enormous "houses of god" called cathedrals. Even in the high-rise, high-tech late 20th century we're still staggered by these structures that were built in low-rise, low-tech medieval times, without the help of any of our modern building aids! They must have seemed nothing short of miraculous when they were first built.

Some extremely uplifting facts about cathedrals

- Cathedrals are sometimes described as "prayers in stone". They were built as a celebration of people's belief in their Christian God.
- People in thriving market towns and cities often built cathedrals as a way of thanking God for making them and their towns prosperous.

- Cathedrals were incredibly expensive. They often took more than 100 years to build and sometimes several generations of builders would be employed on the same job.

- Usually, all the people in a town would muck in and make some sort of a contribution to the project, either by lending a helping hand or giving a donation of money or building materials (a bucket of sand, half a dozen masonry nails, that sort of thing).

I'M DONATING MY HUSBAND AS A MODEL FOR YOUR GARGOYLES

- Cathedrals were sometimes described as the "Bibles of the poor". In the days when they were first built most people couldn't read or write and, to make matters worse – until the late Middle Ages – they couldn't understand a word of the church sermons either, because they were all given in Latin!

- Cathedrals (and some churches) contained stained-glass windows, as well as carvings and tapestries that showed scenes and stories from the Bible – this provided a really good way for people to learn about their religion.

- Cathedrals were like a headquarters for the bishops who ruled over the Christian Church – they often also housed important holy relics (no, not the bishops!) – things like sacred bits of robes and saints' bones.
- The cathedrals towered into the sky with their great spires pointing towards the heavens and God. The spires could be seen from miles and miles around – they weren't hidden by vast office blocks and shopping malls as they sometimes are nowadays. As people went about their daily business they could see the spires wherever they were, and so they were reminded of their faith.
- Unfortunately, as time went on, some people began to get a bit competitive about their cathedrals.

Mind-boggling fact

When Pope Julius II needed money to pay for the rebuilding of the Roman church of St Peter's in 1507, he came up with the bright idea of charging people to let them off their sins. When people went to confess their wrongdoings they were given the choice of saying lots of "Hail Marys" (little prayers) or handing over some cash. These "pay or pray" arrangements were known as "indulgences". So – if someone came to confess to his local priest that he'd forgotten to feed his goldfish, massacred the entire population of Sicily ... or something like that – the priest would say...

All right, I'll let you off this time but you must give us 5,000 lira towards the new building work!

During the 13th century, King Henry III of England wanted to rebuild Westminster Abbey in the same style as a real humdinger of a cathedral that had just been completed at Rheims in northern France. Unfortunately, he was a bit short of cash, so he decided to raise the money by fining people. So, when the husband of the Countess of Lincoln died, the caring King said that he would order her baby son to be permanently taken away from her if she didn't pay £4,000 into the Westminster Abbey rebuilding fund!

Architecture spotting!
Fascinating features to look for in a cathedral

1 Roof bosses Circular clusters of carved stone found at the points on the ceiling where the ribs meet – often beautifully decorated with flower shapes or Bible scenes.

2 Vault Arched underside of the cathedral roof.

3 Rose windows Round windows filled with brilliantly coloured stained glass – looks like the petals of an open flower.

4 Ribs The stone arches that form the strong but lightweight frame that helps support the roof.

5 Tomb effigies Statues (usually lying down) of well-known people – often local and *always* dead.

6 Floor tiles Made from baked clay and decorated with coloured patterns – sometimes arranged in the shape of a maze.

7 Gargoyles Face-shaped spouts direct rainwater away from the cathedral walls – made deliberately ugly to frighten evil spirits. Stone carvers sometimes gave everyone a laugh by making them look just like a well-known bishop or another workman.

8 Flashing Long strips of lead (soft metal) used on the outside of the cathedral to cover the gaps between the roof and walls.

9 Flying buttress *Not* a medieval wrestling move ... doesn't fly either!

How a flying buttress works

1 Narrow and graceful arches support the cathedral walls which are constantly being pushed outwards by the enormous weight of the roof.

2 They transfer the "thrust" of the ceiling away from the walls and into the ground.

3 Said to "fly" because they carry the forces of gravity that pass over the interior of the cathedral.

Something to do – make your own gargoyle

What you need:
some "self-hardening" modelling clay
some modelling tools
a mirror

What to do:
1 Look in the mirror – pull a really horrible "open-mouthed" face.
2 Model the clay into the shape of the face.
3 Make sure there is a hole in the top part of the back of the gargoyle's head to allow the water to pass through to its open mouth.
4 Let the clay set hard.
5 Hold the gargoyle under running water and watch it dribble!

GREAT! BUT WHICH ONE IS THE GARGOYLE?

6 Close your mouth and allow your own face to return to its normal stunningly gorgeous state.

Six great cathedrals to look up to

1 St Paul's Cathedral, London St Paul's is the fifth church to be built on its site (there may even have been a Roman temple there before the first one). Old St Paul's got a bit shabby in the 17th century and wasn't really used as a church. Horse markets took place there, shops were set up, ball games played and a circus horse performed the trick of trotting up the stairs to the bell tower!

50

In 1666, the cathedral was so badly damaged by the Great Fire of London that it had to be rebuilt. Christopher Wren (1632–1723) redesigned St Paul's. "New" St Paul's appeared in a famous Second World War photograph which shows the cathedral standing undamaged during the "Blitz" as all the buildings around it burned. It was said that German bomber pilots used it as a marker.

2 Chartres, France Begun in AD 1195, this cathedral took only 35 years to build and is big enough to hold 18,000 people. Its 173 stained glass windows are thought to be the most beautiful in the world. It also contains 10,000 statues and a veil said to have belonged to the Virgin Mary.

51

3 Durham Cathedral, England Begun in AD 1093 and completed in AD 1133, it was built to house the remains of St Cuthbert (AD 635–687). It used to be surrounded by a ring of wooden crosses. People on the run from the law could go there and claim "sanctuary" – once they'd passed the crosses they could stay there for up to 35 days without being arrested.

A Sunday newspaper recently voted this the finest building in all of Britain – so go and see it!

4 The Cathedral of St John the Divine, New York, USA This cathedral was started in 1892 but it's still not finished. But, part way through construction, it was decided that it would be a much better idea to spend the money on making the lives of local poor people more comfortable, rather than using it to pay for

things like extra flying buttresses, vaulted arches and gargoyles.

THIS IS MY LUNCH PACK OF NOTRE DAME

5 Notre Dame, Paris Built between AD 1163 and 1270, Notre Dame is said to be a great example of a Gothic cathedral. It has pointed arches, flying buttresses, very high ceilings and masses of windows. It is featured in the famous novel *The Hunchback of Notre Dame*. Notre Dame was also a medieval "sanctuary", and during the French Revolution the lead from its roofs was melted to make weapons.

6 Sagrada Familia, Barcelona You'll do a quadruple-take on this one and *still* not believe your eyes! Like a cathedral from the set of a science-fiction movie, it looks as if it's alive. There are flowing shapes and curves everywhere. It has been described as a "stone forest". The architect, Antoni Gaudi (1852–1926), got his inspiration from natural objects like plants, rocks and the sea. Lots of weird shapes appear on the building's surfaces, including leaves, birds, reptiles, fantasy insects and babies.

Begun in 1884, Sagrada Familia is still being built and is not even half finished.

The ideal dome competition

Not all cathedrals are topped with a spire or tower – some, like St Paul's, are covered by a huge dome. During the Renaissance period (14th to 16th centuries AD), the authorities in the city of Florence in Italy wanted to build the biggest dome in the world for their new cathedral.

However, there were a few problems...

In 1417, a competition was organized to find an architect for the ideal dome. One bright spark came up with this idea ... though it wasn't taken up (surprise, surprise!).

Goldsmith and architect, Filippo Brunelleschi (1377–1146), had his own much better idea...

Brunelleschi suggested that all the competitors be asked to stand an egg on its end on a smooth marble surface. Amazingly, the authorities agreed.

The other competitors failed to make their eggs stand up – brainy Filippo simply picked up his egg, smashed one end of it, then stood it up on end.

Filippo had to work with an architect and sculptor called Lorenzo Ghiberti (1378–1455). He wasn't too happy about this because he wanted to be top dog – so he hatched a crafty plot...

Lorenzo was left in charge on his own. Problems arose – the way they always do...

Filippo was asked to return and take complete charge of the building. This is how his mind-boggling idea worked...

● He built a double dome – one inside the other. This reduced the total weight of the large (and incredibly spectacular!) outer dome. The inner dome supported itself and was connected to the larger outer dome by stone ribs.

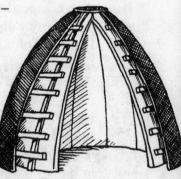

- Even though it was incredibly heavy, the dome kept its shape with the help of huge chains made from iron and stone – it didn't need buttresses.
- Amazing animal-powered hoists (invented by Filippo) lifted materials from ground level to a man-powered crane inside the dome which then raised them to the working area.

- Filippo had restaurants and wine shops built inside the dome so workers wouldn't waste time and energy nipping down to ground level for their dinner.

The dome was started in 1420 and finished in 1434 (that's next to no time in Renaissance building years!).

Mind-boggling religious buildings

1 Borobudur Buddhist Temple, Java, Indonesia

Built in the eighth and ninth centuries AD, it looks like an enormous rectangular wedding cake that's been plonked in the middle of the jungle. Its walled terraces are decorated with thousands of carvings showing scenes from Buddha's life. Abandoned due to local earthquakes and volcanic eruptions, it was rediscovered in 1814. During the 1970s and 80s, a computer was used to record the exact positions of one million stones that were removed for cleaning during a ten-year restoration project.

2 The Royal Mosque of Isfahan, Iran Built in the 17th century by worshippers of the Islamic prophet Mohammed. Instead of having spires or steeples like Christian churches, mosques have incredibly tall towers called minarets from which holy men call Muslims to prayer. When they pray, Muslims must face the holy city of Mecca – the direction is shown by a niche on an inside wall of the mosque. The Islamic

religion does not allow any realistic pictures of people or objects to appear in its art so the temples are decorated with magnificent "abstract" patterns like these ...

3 The Lingaraja Temple, Bhubaneswar, N-E India Built in AD 1000 to the Hindu god of destruction and creation. Each year a statue of a god is carried out of the temple then dipped in the holy water of a nearby lake. The main tower of the temple looks just like an incredibly tall beehive.

4 The Temple of Angkor Wat, Cambodia (Kampuchea) The biggest religious building in the world – built in honour of Hindu god Vishnu in the 12th century then abandoned in 1431 and (amazingly!) "lost" until it was discovered by a 19th-century French explorer who spotted the towers peeping above the rainforest treetops. This is part of a city of temples with room for more than one million people.

5 The Churches of Lalibela, Ethiopia These 11 churches were built in the 12th century. They're just like walk-in sculptures. Each one is chiselled out of solid rock. They are connected by underground tunnels and have sloping floors to allow the torrential summer rains to flow away. One whole church is carved in the shape of a Greek cross.

6 Hagia Sofia, Constantinople (now called Istanbul), Turkey This "heavenly house" has been a Christian church *and* an Islamic mosque – but is now a museum. Built between AD 532 and 537 on orders of Roman Emperor Justinian, Hagia Sofia has a monster dome 30 m (100 ft) across and 50 m (160 ft) high. Roman historian Procopius said it looked as if it was "suspended from heaven on a golden chain". When Istanbul was conquered by the Turks in 1453 they turned the church into a mosque and added four minarets.

Last brick

Building temples and cathedrals to praise gods is serious business – there's no room for mind-boggling mistakes. Architects and builders need careful plans to make sure nothing goes wrong ... during the building or afterwards. However, *some* barmy builders don't think nearly so carefully...

BARMY BUILDERS

Every day, as you make your way to school you will probably see hundreds of buildings and – give or take the odd unhinged door, cracked tile, or chunk of crazy paving – most of them will probably be completely normal. There are some buildings, however, that aren't the slightest bit normal – they're very strange. Many of these batty buildings were constructed in England during the 18th and 19th centuries when extremely wealthy (and completely barmy?) British aristocrats started a craze for building the extremely odd and often totally useless structures known as follies.

How to go building barmy

William Beckford was building barmy. He wasn't born that way – he just developed building mania as he grew up. In 1770, when he was only ten, his father died and left him a sugar plantation in Jamaica, some country houses and (just to make sure the little lad didn't go short of a penny or three) £2,000 *a week* pocket money!

This is how William spent his time (and money) over the next few years...

- He studied music with Mozart.
- He wrote a romantic novel, *Vathek* (highly rated by the famous poet, Lord Byron!).
- He studied building design with a famous architect, Sir George Cozens.
- He travelled around Europe looking at buildings ... in the company of his own personal doctor, his own personal baker (well, have *you* tried buying

an Eccles cake in Barcelona?), five servants, 24 musicians and two dogs – called Mrs Fry and Mrs Fartleberry!

- He got really excited by the monasteries and cathedrals he saw in Spain and Portugal – especially the ones with the extra-tall towers and steeples.
- He returned from his wanderings completely "building barmy" and cried something like...

> *I want a mind-boggling building all of my very own ... with a tower so tall that it will give people nose bleeds just when they think about it!*

... then set about to building himself an abbey with a monster, octagonal (eight-sided) tower on his country estate at Fonthill in Wiltshire.

How to build in the barmy Beckford Manner

1 Have a 15 km (7 mile) long, 4 metre (13 ft) high wall built around your estate to stop nosy parkers peering in at your potty project.

2 Get an architect to design your building then generally ignore his plans and sensible advice about having proper foundations dug for your tower. Be so impulsive and impatient that when you get an idea you want it done yesterday! (Well, he *did* write his novel in just three days!)

3 Use wood and cement as your main materials – they're quicker to build with than stone or brick.

4 Employ 500 labourers and give them lots of beer to drink because you think it will make them work faster (rather than fall over, fight or fall asleep!).

5 Stand back feeling as proud as punch when your 90 metre (300 ft) tall tower is finally finished after six years' work.

6 Feel a bit apprehensive as your brand-new tower begins to wobble ... and teeter ... and sway ... then falls down!

7 Shrug your shoulders, and start all over again – only this time take seven years to build the tower and use some stone to make it stronger!

8 Celebrate the completion of your new tower with a Christmas feast cooked in its kitchens – then listen to the sound of collapsing walls and ceilings as the kitchens cave in before you've even had time to finish your Christmas pud!

9 Start again ... then sell your third tower and the rest of your property because you've got money troubles. Discover soon after the sale that this tower has also collapsed!

10 Build a fourth tower – but have this one built on proper foundations and keep it a bit shorter, at about 40 m (130 ft) so that it might stand the test of time and allow you to give up your towering ambitions for good.

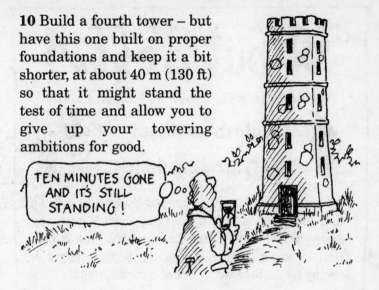

TEN MINUTES GONE AND IT'S STILL STANDING!

Home ... free to good hermit!

Another British landowner and folly fanatic was The Hon. Charles Hamilton. Charles lived on his own country estate at Pain's Hill, Cobham, Surrey in the 18th century. He was dripping with dosh, batty about buildings and potty about paintings, so he tried to recreate his favourite romantic landscapes by filling his 400-acre garden with all sorts of barmy buildings, including: a medieval gazebo (summer-house), a Gothic temple, a Greek temple (made from papier-mâché!), a ruined abbey (how do you *build* a "ruined" abbey?), a huge Roman arch, a castle tower, a Turkish tent and a Chinese bridge. As a finishing touch he also built a rather cosy two-storey hermitage, complete with en-suite meditation chamber – all he needed now was a pet hermit to put in it ... so, he advertised for one!

What Folly!

The magazine for the Wally With the Lolly

Situations Vacant

WANTED - ONE HERMIT

Are you fond of your own company? Keen to get into some really serious neglect of your personal grooming and hygiene? Fancy reading the same book (yes, just the one!) for seven years? If so you may be the person I'm looking for … because … I need a hermit, *now*!

Job description Shunning human race – reading Bible – pondering.

Hermitage and hermitting kit provided – Bible, hassock (to pray on), comfy mat (to lay on) … plus food and water.

Salary £700 payable on completion of seven years' successful hermitting. Attractive free uniform – traditional hermit's camel hair robe (nice and itchy!). Please note – traditional and ludicrously long hermit's beard and fingernails *not* supplied – applicant must grow own. Cutting – or even sneaky nibbling! – of nails, or hair, will result in non-payment of *all* wages!

Apply to: The Honourable Charles Hamilton, Pain's Hill, Cobham, Surrey.

Despite the generous conditions and wages on offer only one person applied for the job (perhaps there was a hermit shortage at the time?).

After three weeks of sitting in the hermitage thinking deep (and meaningless?) thoughts the hermit went off to the pub and was never seen again (well, not by the Hon. Charles, anyway).

The secret life of a dedicated mole

It's a pity that William John Cavendish Bentinck Scott, the fifth Duke of Portland (1800–1879) wasn't around to apply for that hermit's job. After all, he was very fond of his own company ... and absolutely *no one* else's! The Duke was incredibly rich ... but also incredibly shy! So what did he do? Go on a self-assertiveness training course? Buy himself a power wig, some shades and a mega-cool sports stagecoach? No, of course he didn't! He decided to build a vast underground hidey-hole beneath his home at Welbeck Abbey in Nottinghamshire. Some of the things he had built or altered to ensure his privacy are almost beyond belief. See if you can work out which are false and which are true.

What he had built ...
1 24 kilometres (15 miles) of gas-lit, underground tunnels, including one nearly two kilometres (one-mile) long. It led from his coach house to the edge of

his enormous estate. When the Duke wanted to go to London he was driven through the tunnel, then to the station where his coach was then loaded onto a flat railway wagon (with him still inside). TRUE/FALSE

2 A huge underground ballroom, 53 metres (174 ft) in length – big enough to hold 2,000 people. It was never used because the Duke was too shy to invite anyone to a knees-up. TRUE/FALSE

3 Underground libraries full of books which he never read. TRUE/FALSE

4 An underground billiards room big enough for 12 tables – which were never played on! TRUE/FALSE

5 An underground railway that went from the estate kitchens to his living quarters. This was for his daily roast chicken to travel on – when it was ready, the cook would pop it into its own specially heated little truck and send it to the Duke's dining-room. TRUE/FALSE

6 A huge above-ground riding school for 100 horses

... but *without* any windows (surely he didn't think the *horses* were shy too!). Actually, the horses were never ridden – neither by the Duke nor anyone else – most of the time they stayed in their stables. TRUE/FALSE

...and a few of the alterations he had done

1 Almost every room in the estate's main building (Welbeck Abbey itself) was stripped of its antique furniture, valuable carpets and paintings. The Duke ordered them to be dumped in a storage area then had the empty rooms painted shocking pink. He also had a toilet installed in the middle of each one. TRUE/FALSE

2 He had double letterboxes – one for "in" and one for "out" – put in the doors of his living-rooms so that he wouldn't have to come face to face with his servants – they communicated by notes pushed through the slots. TRUE/FALSE

THE DUKE HAS 100 HORSES, BUT HE NEVER RIDES THEM

HE PROBABLY CAN'T FIND THEM WITHOUT THE WINDOWS!

3 Even his doctor had to talk to him through a closed door. This obviously made physical examinations very difficult indeed. TRUE/FALSE

NOW YOUR GRACE ...PLEASE SAY AAH!

4 There was so much building activity going on at Welbeck that at one time it was reported that the Duke had 15,000 builders working for him. He treated his workers very well – as well as paying them a good wage he also gave each of them an umbrella ... and a donkey to come to work on! TRUE/FALSE

Answers: All true

The most exclusive "high" school in the world

Are you like the Duke? Do you get fed up with the company of other people, especially the incredibly irritating types that you have to go to school with? You know, the ones who are sometimes referred to as "the other children"! If you do, you may wish you had a dad like William Latimer.

In 1549, William built a six-storey brick tower on his estate near Orford in Suffolk, England as a private school for his daughter Ellen – it was so private that she attended it all on her own! The competition was tough, though! It wasn't easy staying on top. On Mondays she was always bottom of the class (rooms) but as the week progressed, she worked her way up – and by Sunday she always ended up "top of the school"! This was Ellen's actual timetable for the week!

Windows of opportunity

At least Ellen had windows to gaze out of if lessons got boring. When Lytham Hall in Lancashire was built, between 1752 and 1759, artists were employed to paint pretend windows in many of the places where the real ones should have been. Why?

a) It was the daft idea of yet another building barmy aristocrat.

b) To fool burglars.

c) The British government had introduced a "window tax".

Architecture spotting!

Look out for "blank" windows on older buildings – they may well have been bricked up to avoid the 18th-century window tax. Perhaps you could do the owners of the buildings a favour by getting an adult to tell them that it's now all right to have the real things reinstalled – the tax was abolished in 1851!

Five foolish follies

1 Fuller's Pyramid

A wealthy 19th-century landowner and MP known as Mad Jack Fuller had this 6 m (20 ft) tall pyramid built in the churchyard at Rose Hill in Sussex, England. He gave instructions that he should be buried inside it sitting at a table wearing his top hat, with a bottle of wine

NO CORKSCREW!

in his hand and a roast chicken set out in front of him (but only when he was dead, of course!). He also said that he wanted broken glass to be strewn all around him to "keep away the devil" (who would obviously be really desperate to pinch his roast chicken!).

2 The Triangular Lodge

Built in 1593 in Rushton, Northants, by Sir Thomas Tresham. Sir Thomas obviously thought that the best things in life are three, so he built this three-sided folly – which also has three storeys, three windows on each side of each storey, three rows of three, three-sided pinnacles and three lots of almost anything else you care to think of!

3 Another pyramid – Farley Down, Hampshire

This was erected by Mr Paulet St John as a monument to his horse. Mr St John was out riding the horse when the ground gave way in front of them. The quick-thinking steed made an 8 m (25 ft) leap over the chasm and saved both of their lives. When the heroic horse – which he renamed "Beware Chalk Pit" – finally died, he buried it in a large pyramid-shaped tomb.

4 Burton Pynsent Column, Somerset

This tall column with a spiral staircase inside was closed after an inquisitive cow wandered into it, climbed the staircase then plunged to its death.

5 Faringdon Folly

A tall tower designed and built in 1935 by Lord Berners and meant to be "entirely useless". He put a notice on it which said...

MEMBERS OF THE PUBLIC COMMITTING SUICIDE FROM THIS TOWER DO SO AT THEIR OWN RISK

Hopefully, this gave any potential suicides such a good laugh that they changed their minds!

True grout!

It was not just eccentric 18th- and 19th-century English aristocrats who built fabulous follies for which they are now remembered. Simon Rhodia was born in 1879 in Rome and moved to America in 1891. He earned his living repairing telephones and setting tiles and was poor for most of his life. He said that to be remembered after you were long gone from the world you had to be "good good" … or "bad bad". He also said, "I had in mind to do something big, and I did!" He did – he decided to build something that was very "tall tall" and extremely "noticeable noticeable"! So…

Without using drawing-board plans, building machinery or scaffolding – just his tiler's tools and a window cleaner's belt – he began to build.

He built lots of towers from bits of pipework, some as high as 30 m (100 ft). He decorated them with the thousands of old tiles, dishes and bottles and seashells that he collected.

When his incredible towers were finally finished in 1954 – after 33 years of building – he gave them away to one of his neighbours and left town for good!

Ghostbuster – a very spooky story!

Sarah Winchester and her husband, Oliver, were a happily married couple – they had a bouncing baby boy and were also very rich – so they wanted for nothing. Oliver's father had made a fortune from making and selling the famous "Winchester" Repeating Rifle – the gun that was supposed to have won the Wild West of America. Unfortunately, it was also used to kill thousands of native Americans plus quite a few other unlucky individuals.

In 1881 Sarah's happy life was shattered by two terrible tragedies. First, Oliver died and then her baby son died also. Poor Sarah, suddenly and cruelly left alone, was absolutely devastated by these events so she went to see a spiritualist (someone who claims they can contact the souls of dead people) for comfort and advice.

"You have suffered these dreadful misfortunes because you are being haunted!" said the spiritualist, after hearing her story.

"Oh that's terrible," cried Sarah. "But, why would a ghost want to haunt me? I've done nothing to upset anyone."

I'M AFRAID YOU'VE MISUNDERSTOOD ME, MRS WINCHESTER, YOU AREN'T JUST BEING HAUNTED BY ONE GHOST, YOU'RE BEING HAUNTED BY HUNDREDS OF THEM, MAYBE THOUSANDS!

Sarah's face went pale and she gasped helplessly, completely lost for words. "It's true," continued the spiritualist, "I can feel it in my bones. The ghosts of all the people killed by the rifles that made the Winchester fortune are now seeking their revenge. You, I'm afraid, are their target!"

76

Sarah was distraught – well you would be, wouldn't you, if you'd just been told that a whole army of spooks was after you? What could she do? Well, if the ghosts were going to persecute her the least she could do was make it difficult for them. She decided to bamboozle the spooks by creating a mind-boggling building and set about spending the Winchester fortune on turning her whole house in San Jose, California, into an enormous "ghost trap"!

She had enormous extensions built – dozens and dozens of rooms added – hundreds of extra windows put in and masses of maze-like corridors installed. It didn't stop there! To really spook the spooks she got the builders to put in staircases that went nowhere, and new doors that just opened on to blank walls.

"I'll sleep in a different room each night!" she thought. "That'll get the ghosts so confused that they'll become completely lost – then give up haunting me for ever!"

The ghost-trap idea got such a grip on Sarah that she just couldn't stop having additions made to the house and she continued her mission for the rest of her life. By the time she was an old lady, her house had an amazing total of: 160 rooms, 2,000 doors, 13 bathrooms, 47 fireplaces, 40 staircases – and 10,000 windows. Her servants had to use maps to find their way around!

ER...COULD YOU SHOW ME THE WAY OUT ? I ONLY CAME IN TO READ THE METER... AND THAT WAS 15 YEARS AGO!

THAT'S NOTHING! I'VE BEEN A LOST SOUL EVER SINCE THE MASSACRE AT COYOTE CREEK!

When she died in 1922, Sarah's "ghostbusting" mansion – Winchester House – had become so huge that it covered two-and-a-half hectares (six acres), about the size of four primary schools. A brilliant place to play hide and seek in – just as long as you're not afraid of ghosts!

Did it work?
Sarah did manage to survive, but, in 1906, during the great San Francisco earthquake (see page 120) a very strange thing happened. Sarah was trapped in one of the very rooms she'd built to baffle the banshees, and almost died! The tremors from the quake caused the door of the room to jam shut and, at first, her cries for help went unheard. Because of the size of her mansion, it took her servants absolutely ages to locate her and they only discovered her in the nick of time – she was reported

to be on the point of starving to death. Just a coincidence ... or another spooky attempt at revenge?

Last brick

Are batty buildings like Faringdon Folly and Rhodia's Towers completely useless – or have those batty builders done architecture fans a big favour by erecting their stunning structures? Follies and other unusual buildings may look startling at first sight – but it's fun to look out for them on long and boring car journeys. Seeing something built for fun is definitely more enjoyable than staring at unimaginative monstrosities – built only to make money – don't you think?

LOONY LOCATIONS

People don't just put up potty buildings, they also choose the looniest of locations to build them, like underground, on stilts, in rock faces, up trees, or even in swamps situated in the middle of lakes with no building materials to be had for miles around...

Tenochtitlan – built by Aztecs
DESTROYED BY RUFFNECKS

The Aztecs – who lived in Mexico between the 13th and 16th centuries – were a savage and bloodthirsty people, fond of ripping out the still-beating hearts of their enemies and waving them around like bargains at the January sales. As a result of this, they were rarely invited to barbecues or wine and cheese parties by the other Central American tribes

AN EAGLE WITH A SERPENT ON A CACTUS...COULD THIS BE THE SIGN WE SEEK?

LET'S HOPE SO MY FEET ARE KILLING ME

THE GOD HAVE CHO THIS LAKE OUR NEW

and were forced to spend most of their days wandering around Mexico with no proper home of their own.

Their god – whose name was Huitzilopochtli – told them that they must roam about until they found an eagle sitting on a cactus eating a serpent next to a place where fish swam – and this would be the place where they should build their home. After at least a hundred years of wandering around, the aimless Aztecs finally found what they were looking for.

The site they chose to make their settlement on was a very unpromising looking bit of land in the middle of a lake. They called it Tenochtitlan – which means "place of the prickly pear cactus". It wasn't going to be an easy spot to build a huge city – the ground was extremely soft and swampy – and, more to the point, they didn't have anything to build it with! Nevertheless, the Aztecs

COULD WE HAVE A SECOND OPINION?

THE FIRST THING WE DO IS OPEN UP A CANOE SHOP

RIGHT!

AT LEAST OUR NEW HOME COMES WITH RUNNING WATER!

persevered with the project and, after bartering for building materials with their neighbours, the Tepanecs, they got to work. After a couple of hundred years of construction work they had transformed the island on the lake into an incredible city full of richly decorated buildings, beautiful bridges, awesome aqueducts, shimmering waterways and magnificent gardens overflowing with fragrant flowers, trees and shrubs. One of the first Europeans to clap eyes on Tenochtitlan was so astounded by its beauty that he had to pinch himself to make sure he was fully awake. The gobsmacked Spaniard later said...

Gazing at such wonderful sights, we did not know what to say ... or whether what appeared before us was real! ... Are not the things we see a dream?

Important Az'technical info

- By the end of the 15th century the city covered an area of 1,000 hectares and had an estimated population of a quarter of a million people – which was absolutely enormous for those days. Even the great cities of Europe at that time had no more than 120,000 inhabitants.
- The Aztecs made their buildings from adobe (baked mud) or stone – many of them had to be supported by long poles in order to prevent them from disappearing into the mud of the island.

- The island was criss-crossed by a network of canals – these were the main "streets" of Tenochtitlan. They divided the city into blocks. The Aztecs often travelled around their city by barge and canoe.

- It's been estimated that Tenochtitlan contained 360 temples – the biggest and poshest of these was built in the 15th century in the centre of the city and was known as The Great Temple. In 1487, when this pyramid-shaped building was finally complete, the Aztecs decided to have a spectacular opening ceremony at which their priests beheaded 20,000 sacrificial victims then rolled their bodies down the temple steps.

- Quite near to the Great Temple there was a building called "The Skull Rack" – a bit like the vegetable rack in a supermarket, but with the severed heads of sacrificial victims piled up on it, instead of cabbages and onions!

- It's quite remarkable that the Aztecs managed to build their great city at all – they had no iron tools, no wheels, no ploughs, no carts, no horses (and no three-speed hammer drills with snap on grinding and sanding attachments). They really were "low-tech Aztecs".

Time's up for Tenochtitlan

In 1519, the Spanish adventurer and explorer, Hernan Cortès (1485–1547) arrived at the great city of Tenochtitlan. Hernan was on a sort of fact-finding expedition for the rulers of Spain. His mission was to discover new territories and sources of wealth (...then steal them).

Postcard to - King Charles of Spain
from - Hernan Cortes, Mexico, 1519.

Your Majesty

Journey not too bad, although the Caribbean sea gets quite choppy at times. ~~sea~~ sea sick Landed at Veracruz and immediately burned boats, just to show the lads that I really am a hard commander. me looking hard!
Have arrived at an amazing city called ~~Tenoctitlan~~ ~~Tenostitlan~~ Tenochtitlan. It's ace.
Me and the fellas think it's even more wonderful than our own city of Granada. The locals think I'm some sort of god, so we're being treated quite well.
Went round to Montezuma's place for a meal last night (he's the Aztec emperor). Good news, had roast turkey, bad news, it was covered in chocolate sauce. Feel dead yucky now, but don't try ← this! I am still looking forward to going to put on the big show the Aztecs are going to put on for us today, something to do with hearts, I think....

Best Wishes (Plus all the grovelly stuff)

Hernan

← me   Montezuma →

As the ingenious Aztecs proved, just because a building site looks a bit unpromising at first doesn't mean that it can't be turned into a "des. res." (estate agent language for "desirable residence") as you'll discover, when you read about...

Daunting ... but desirable dwellings
The Tree House at Pitchford Hall, Shropshire
A des. res. built in the branches of a huge lime tree in the grounds of a stately home 300 years ago (and still standing!) – said to have been lived in by Lady Sybil Grant in the early 1900s when she moved out of Pitchford Hall because she couldn't stand the

sound of nearby rushing water and was also terrified of the haunted graveyard next door.

Venice, Italy Founded about AD 400 when fishermen fled to marshy islands in a saltwater lake to escape the barbarians who were invading Italy from northern Europe. The islands soon became overcrowded, so the fishermen pushed poles into the seabed, extended the islands with piles of stones and planks, then began building on the resulting artificial platforms.

Today the city is built on 118 islands, which are criss-crossed by a network of 100 canals and more than 400 bridges. Not to be missed is the Bridge of Sighs. This leads to a jail. It got its name because the prisoners being led across it sighed at the prospect of being locked away (and missing all that beautiful architecture).

The Cave Dwellings of Cappadocia, Turkey
Hundreds of cone-shaped shelters carved out of a huge rocky hillside by monks between the fourth and tenth centuries AD. The shelters were later joined by tunnels to form an enormous "honeycomb" that linked over 300 monasteries and churches! Many of the interior walls of the churches are covered with colourful religious paintings. It has been estimated that up to as many as 30,000 people may have used the churches.

The "Rose" City of Petra, Jordan This fantastic ancient city is hidden in a steep-sided ravine (canyon). The beautiful buildings are actually carved out of the rosy-red cliff face and the rooms reach far back into the rock. It's just as impressive as the most fantastic temples and palaces in the world. Abandoned after the fourth century AD but rediscovered in 1812.

Port Moresby, New Guinea Dozens of houses standing on enormous pillars, or stilts, in the sea – each support is made from an entire tree trunk! Space saving and very popular with anglers, this is a building style favoured throughout tropical countries. It's used on land, too, where it provides storage space and keeps out damp, snakes, creepy-crawlies.

The Underwater "Smoking" Room, England This was built at Whitley Park in Surrey in the late 1890s. It's a dome-shaped room (a bit like an enormous underwater conservatory), constructed on the bed of a lake and reached by a 122 m (400 ft) long tunnel. Rich (and potty?) businessman, Whitaker Wright, liked to puff at a cigar or three in here amongst the potted palms, whilst observing life at the bottom.

Now you see it ... now you don't!

An agricultural contractor called Trevor Sedgebeer converted a barn to a two-storey house but didn't bother to get "planning permission" for it (that's something you have to get from the local council if you want to erect a new building or change the look of an existing one). When the local authorities found out, they insisted that Trevor should knock his house down. So what do you think Trevor did next?

a) He knocked the house down.

b) He knocked the planning officers down.

c) He removed the whole of the top floor of the house then hid the remaining single-storey bit under earth and grass so that it looked as if the whole building had been demolished.

Answer: c). After turning his house into a bungalow, Trevor covered it with turf so that it was completely hidden from sight. He then built a trapdoor in the "grassy bank" so that he could get in and out of his secret home. Believe it or not

EVERYTHING SEEMS
TO BE IN ORDER
MR SEDGEBEER

... his plan worked (well, for a while, anyway). Despite visiting him many times the planning officers didn't suspect that he'd bunged his bungalow into a bunker!

Last brick

It's amazing what mind-boggling builders can come up with when they really put their minds (and hands) to it. Maybe difficult challenges bring out the best in them! It certainly did with the people who built Venice. Many mind-boggling building fans think it's the most beautiful city in the world – the only problem is, 12 million of them go there every year to admire its awesome architecture and in the summer months the whole place becomes packed to bursting. Perhaps it's time for some brave builders to find a few more loony locations?

POSH PALACES & MIND-BOGGLING MANSIONS

Most of us live in fairly comfortable homes with two or three bedrooms, a sitting room, bathroom, and kitchen and think we're quite lucky to be there. Some people live in luxurious mansions with so many rooms, they probably wouldn't notice if you and your family moved into the East Wing.

People live in posh palaces and mind-boggling mansions for all sorts of reasons. Sometimes they're just born into them because they happen to be a member of a ruling family...

...and sometimes they've had them specially created because they're the sort of person who has just got to have the best of absolutely *everything* ... like W.R. Hearst!

Imagine what it would be like if you could build the house of your dreams! That's exactly what the American businessman, William Randolph Hearst (1863–1951), did in California earlier this century. William's dad had made a vast fortune by discovering huge amounts of really valuable stuff like gold and coal hidden underground.

When his dad died, William inherited his huge fortune and, as if that wasn't enough, he went on to make even more money by starting up newspapers. Eventually, he decided to build an amazing home on a hill at St Simeon in California.

Hearst Castle – staggering facts about a staggering structure

1 Hearst Castle took 27 years to build and cost $30 million. It has over 100 rooms including its own cinema, two libraries, a grand assembly hall and a garage big enough for 25 limousines! It's also known as "Casa Grande" – that's Spanish for "big house" ... no prizes for guessing why.

2 While his house was being built, Mr Hearst had set about acquiring a few interesting bits and pieces to give it a touch of class. He didn't pop down to the local DIY store, however – he sent an army of agents all round the world to find him fabulous fittings with a difference ... at *any* price.

3 At times, when a room had just been added to the building at phenomenal expense, he'd taken one look at it, then said something like, "Knock it down and start again – now!" and the poor builders had had to do exactly that.

4 He had two mammoth swimming pools built: an

outdoor pool, made of marble, which has a Greek temple next to it; and an indoor pool lined with so many Venetian glass tiles that it took four years to lay them all. (By the way, the indoor pool has two full-size tennis courts built on top of it.) Mr Hearst also had a complete monastery shipped over from Spain – stone by stone – but left the whole thing in its packing case when he couldn't decide what to do with it.

5 To give his monster mansion that cosy, homely feel, he had nearly 100 different species of wild animals wandering around Casa Grande. Just to make sure the big hungry ones, like the lions and the bears, didn't eat the small ones, he put them in special pits.

6 If you're the sort of show-off who's got a head the size of the Rocky Mountains, you're going to need to flaunt your fitted features, aren't you? Which is probably why Mr Hearst regularly invited superstar actors to spend a few days away from it all in his sumptuous bedrooms or one of the three luxury cottages he had built in the grounds. And just to make that memorable first impression, Mr High-and-Mighty Hearst was whizzed to meet his guests from his living quarters in a hidden lift and then suddenly appeared from under the ground … as if by magic!

William might appear to have been just a little bit extravagant but, next to King Louis XIV of France, he probably would have appeared positively penny pinching, shy and retiring – Casa Grande might well have been mistaken for the garden shed if it was plonked in the grounds of the Palace of Versailles...

The Mind Boggling Buildings Visitor's Guide to

The Palace of Versailles

Claims to fame?
● The largest palace in Europe.
● Power base of French kings.
● Capital of France between 1682 and 1789.
● The place where battling countries signed the Treaty of Versailles to end the First World War in 1919.

Where is it? Twenty-three km (10 miles) south-west of Paris, France.

Whose idea was it? Louis XIV of France (1638–1715) – otherwise known as "Le Roi Soleil" ("The Sun King") – who, in 1668, decided to turn his father's modest hunting lodge into something a bit more comfortable.

Why was he called the Sun King? After being

made king of France, he came to the conclusion that he was as powerful as the sun!

Who built it? 3,000 builders and 6,000 horses – the builders put up the stonework and the horses did all the fetching and carrying.

How long did it take to build? Forty-seven years.

Any problems then? *Oui, beaucoup!* The whole place was built on fine sandy soil that caused some of the foundations to sink. Many of the builders were forced to work there against their will and never received a proper wage. Hundreds of them died on the job, either by accident, or from fever caught from the surrounding swamps. Louis was *very* upset about the whole thing.

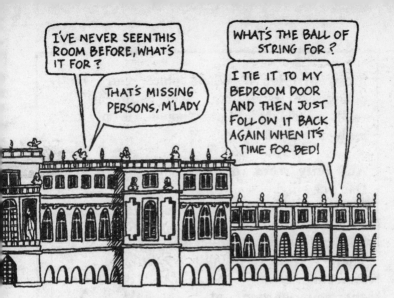

So did he introduce free luncheon vouchers and a health and safety at work policy? No, he just banned everyone from mentioning the deaths and injuries!

Anyone live there, apart from Louis? Yes, his family and 9,000 soldiers, 4,000 servants and 1,000 French aristocrats plus a few other odds and bods – a total of 20,000 people in all. "Le Roi Soleil" liked to have his nobles all in one place where he could keep an eye on them.

How many rooms? There were 1,300 altogether. The whole place is so enormous that the nobles were carried from room to room in sedan chairs (special chairs carried by porters called chairmen).

Main problems? Whole place *really, really* pongy. No proper loos ... or bathrooms! Not really a problem for Louis though! He only had a bath once a year!

And only went to the toilet once a year? Don't be silly!

Any other features?
The Palace Fountains There were 1,400 fountains in the enormous gardens at Versailles – they used more water than was available for all of Paris (which was a pity really, because the poor Parisians regularly suffered from diseases  carried by water and could have done with an extra drop or two). A great machine, consisting of 14 huge waterwheels and more than 200 pumps, was built by 30,000 of the King's soldiers to draw water to the fountains from the River Seine. It was constantly breaking down.

The Hall of Mirrors (Galerie Des Glaces) Huge hall, 72 m (233 ft) long where the Sun King would appear to his courtiers. Enormous mirrors lined the whole of one wall reflecting the light from massive chandeliers, their 3,000 candles and the windows opposite – no doubt giving the courtiers the impression that Louis really was "Le Roi Soleil".

Versailles was a bit like a huge five-star holiday camp and theme park for bored aristocrats. If they grew tired of watching the King eating they could visit the menagerie and marvel at the wild beasts – attend the on-site opera house or theatre – go for a gondola ride on the Grand Canal – tune in to the cool sounds of the water-powered organ in the Grotto de Thetis, or just go for a stroll round the massive 101 hectare (250 acre) gardens and bask in the radiance of the four million flower bulbs that the King imported from Holland every year.

The Empress strikes back

Once upon a time there was a wicked Empress who ruled over a huge, frozen Empire full of poor and hungry people. She was a ruthless and cold-hearted woman who couldn't bear anyone to disobey her. One day, one of the handsome young princes who lived in the Empire enraged the Empress by marrying the love of his life without first seeking the royal ratbag's permission.

"How dare he!" fumed the Empress, when she was told of the marriage, "I will make sure that he lives to regret his mistake for ever more!"

Sadly, not long after the prince's wedding, his new bride died – and he was heartbroken. The Empress seized her chance for revenge and ordered the poor man to become her court jester. But this was not enough – she had a much, much crueller punishment in store. She summoned the cleverest Royal architect to her chambers.

"I want you to design me an ice palace!" she snapped.

"Of course Your Highness!" snivelled the architect. "It will be no problem." It was the coldest winter the Empire had suffered for 30 years – even the mightiest and most turbulent of rivers had been ice-bound for months. Some people had even reported seeing birds stuck up in the air, frozen completely solid in mid-flight!

The architect immediately sent for the best craftsmen and the strongest labourers in the land and set them working on the fantastic frozen folly. They cut huge building blocks from the purest ice they could find and joined them with water so that they were instantly frozen into seamless walls of sparkling crystal.

The ice palace was tremendous – it had windows made from sliced ice, and, in the bedroom, there was even a four-poster bed made from ice, complete with ice mattress, ice quilt, ice pillows and two little ice nightcaps.

In the garden there were ice trees with ice birds, ice cannon that actually fired and, most amazingly of all, a full-sized elephant and rider made entirely from ice.

The Empress was delighted and was now ready to carry out the second bit of her plan. She called the prince to her and introduced him to a poor palace serving girl, whom many people considered to be not particularly nice looking but actually was … in a way it takes a bit of time to appreciate. She told him he must marry the girl.

"Hnrrrrrrgh! … Hrrumph! Cripes!" gasped the astonished couple. But the Empress wasn't finished yet – she now played her master card!

"You will take your honeymoon in the ice palace!" she hissed, her eyes glittering coldly as she savoured the expressions of horror frozen on the faces of her victims!

Just as the tyrant had promised, the couple were married and immediately whisked off to the ice palace. They were then made to sleep in the ice four-poster bed – where they were constantly exposed to the mocking stares of the Empress and her sniggering hangers-on through the transparent walls. It made absolutely no difference trying to pull their ice blankets over their heads and hide under them, for as you know – they too were transparent! The pathetic prince's humiliation was complete.

However, nothing lasts for ever and, when spring came, the incredible ice palace began to melt. Its doorways dripped, its walls wilted, and its domes dribbled and quite soon it was nothing more than a big wet patch on the grass.

The ice palace wasn't the only thing to wither and shrink that year – some time afterwards, the frosty heart of the Empress ticked its last tock and she died.

But what of the pathetic prince and his bride? Well, as the ice palace was shrinking, a warm love began to grow between the prince and the serving girl. By the time the fabulous frosted folly had been reduced to nothing more than a few paddling

pools full of lukewarm water, they were well and truly in love with each other – and they didn't even have to get married because they already were! So, all that was left for them was to live happily ever after – which they did!

They would, wouldn't they. They always do in fairy stories – and this was a fairy tale, wasn't it?

Well no, it wasn't – most of the events in this amazing story are said to have actually happened in Russia during the 18th century. The fiend in a frock was Anna Ivanovna, Empress of all the Russias (1693–1740), the artful architect was Peter Eropkin, and the prince was Michael Alexievich Golitsyn.

Note: The bit about the birds being frozen in mid-air might just be a bit of an exaggeration.

More frozen follies

Ice palaces aren't just something that are built as part of the wicked schemes of evil empresses...

- In January 1986 an ice palace was built at St Paul, Minnesota, USA, using 9,000 blocks of ice. It was 37 m by 27 m (120 ft by 90 ft) and was nearly 40 m (130 ft) high – that's as tall as a 13-storey building!

- At the 1992 Sapporo Snow Festival in Japan 2,720 soldiers built a 13 m (45 ft) high replica of the White House – the official residence of the President of America – entirely out of ice!

Pompous palaces

FIDDLER, DIDDLER AND TWISTER ESTATE AGENTS
PALACE DEPARTMENT

offer an exciting opportunity to acquire the following fine properties...

THE ALHAMBRA PALACE

"Ooh Aah Alhambra!" is what we say here at F, D and T – it's fabulous!

Location Granada, southern Spain

Built between 1238 and 1358

Previous owners Moorish princes from North Africa who ruled Spain for several centuries.

"Moor" than meets the eye From the outside it looks like your average, everyday, enormous

104

medieval castle but inside it's like something out of an Arabian Nights fairy tale because it's got...

- Secluded courtyards with fountains and fragrant rose bushes that bloom all year round.

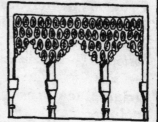

- Arched windows and colonnades decorated with delicate lace-like plasterwork.

- Tiled walls, dazzlingly designed.

- Many stunning rooms of great historical interest, including: The Hall of Abencerrajes – in which a previous owner had all the sons of his first wife beheaded. Purchasers: please do not let this put you off; he mopped up afterwards.

BRIGHTON PAVILION

Agent's note Would suit thrusting young executive couple fond of paddling, night-life, and seagulls, who are looking for a home with a difference.

Location Brighton, Sussex. Sea – three minutes. London – just a short speeding offence away.

Previous owner George, Prince of Wales (later became King George IV).

Overall style A bit of everything but mainly "oriental" – that is, has an Indian and Chinese feel to it.

Original features include:

- gas lights in the shape of dragons
- fake banana tree on dining room ceiling
- silk wall hangings
- lotus petal lamps

… and lots, lots more.

Kitchen Big enough for 12 cooks and their helpers to work in at the same time. Enormous spit for roasting huge chunks of meat ingeniously powered by heat from the fire rising up the chimney. Ceiling supported by huge iron and copper columns that look just like palm trees. The famous chef, Anton Carème (who invented "caramel") served up a button-bursting banquet consisting of 112 different dishes from here!

Bathroom With marble and mahogany (hard, reddish-brown wood) fittings and water pumped direct from the sea.

Fab Music Room So beautiful that George

burst into tears when he first saw it. He played the cello in it and got famous musicians like Rossini to do private gigs here. Badly damaged by a tower that crashed through the roof when it was blown down in the "Great Storm" of 1987.

Outside Lots of minarets (narrow towers) with beautiful "onion"-shaped domes.

THE PALACE OF ISTANA NURUL IMAN
Location Brunei, South-east Asia.
Building work completed 1984.
Current owner The Sultan of Brunei (probably the richest man in the world).
Accommodation Not really room to describe it all here – let's just say that DIY enthusiasts will need to set aside a couple of weekends for decorating as it's got 1,778 rooms!

THERE'S ONLY 167 TOILETS THAT NEED UNBLOCKING

Very "conveniently" appointed It has 257 lavatories (the only way you're going to get

> caught short is by spending too long deciding
> which one to use!).
> **Absolutely enormous underground garage**
> Well, the Sultan has got to have somewhere to
> park his 110 cars!

Last brick

Nowadays you don't have to be a power-crazed king
or a big-headed billionaire to get to see inside many
of these mind-boggling mansions. You just have to
be a traveller with an enquiring mind and a lively
imagination. If you can afford the entrance charge,
you can have a brilliant chance to experience the
sort of place that was once forbidden territory – and
perhaps even imagine, for a while, that it's yours!

FORBIDDING FORTRESSES

Some of the most mind-boggling buildings ever built were constructed because people wanted to show the world how *tough* they were – and to keep out their neighbours. (Especially if they were the kind of neighbours who are forever nipping round to borrow a cup of sugar, slaughter your best herd of pedigree cattle and cut your throat.) In days gone by there was no point in putting up a "KEEP OUT – I LIVE HERE" sign, featuring a picture of the cat wearing your Uncle Percy's false teeth to frighten away unwelcome visitors. If you were serious about keeping out troublemakers what you needed was an enormous fortress – such as Krak des Chevaliers...

A hard fort to krak

Krak des Chevaliers – which means Crag of the Knights – was a Middle Ages superfortress situated in the country now known as Syria. The well-known action-man of the Middle East, Lawrence of Arabia, said that Krak was...

The most admirable castle in the world.

The fort was originally built by the Arabs but was later taken over and rebuilt by Christians during the Wars of the Crusades against the Muslim forces known as the Saracens in the 12th and 13th centuries AD. It was controlled by the Knights of St John – they're the ones who now run that really

109

helpful voluntary ambulance service which you may have seen at sports events and country fairs. The Saracens, who fought against the Christians, were desperate to get into the Krak but the knights managed to hold out against them for over 180 years.

In 1271, the Saracens eventually did manage to crack the Krak. This is how it happened: the Knights were fooled into giving up the castle by a forged letter which the crafty Saracens sent to them by carrier pigeon. The note – which was made to look like it had come from their Christian commanders – said something like...

> *Dear Knights*
> *Listen Lads, give in to the Saracens right this minute, all right? They're not such bad sorts after all!*
> *Best Wishes the Boss*

The krak'ing details
- Accommodation for 2,000 fighting men.
- Built on huge rocky outcrop – therefore making it impossible for potential invaders to ...

a) tunnel under the walls

b) find anywhere to lean their ladders or position their siege machinery, and

c) climb them without being splattered by boulders or drenched in boiling water dropped from above.

- A covered entrance passageway, kept dark at all times, so that any invaders who managed to get into it would be blinded by the sun as they emerged.

- "Zigzag" pathway leading up the rock face to the main entrance. To follow the path, all invaders have to cross and recross the defenders' line of fire.

- Massive outward sloping ramparts (defensive walls) and vast chambers where you can store enough water and grain to last you for years of sieges.

111

Castles in the air

Not all forbidding fortresses are built to keep out enemies – some are created as places where their owners can live out their wildest dreams. King Ludwig II of Bavaria (1845–1886) came from an art-loving family ... but many people thought he took his love for art too far! He was obsessed about the opera music of Richard Wagner, because it filled his head with fantastic thoughts of medieval knights and damsels in distress. He once paid Wagner so much money that it had to be carried home from the bank in two horse-drawn cabs! Ludwig was pretty weird in other ways, too. He liked to have dinner at ten minutes past midnight, and then go for wild sleigh rides in the early hours of the morning.

WHAEEEEEEE!

Ludwig went just as wild when it came to building incredible castles – just for himself – where he could indulge his very wild dreams. His most impressive creation was Neuschwanstein Castle, which took 17 years to construct. The builders used dynamite to blast away the top of a mountain to provide the perfect pitch for Ludwig's dream castle.

The castle wasn't designed by an architect, it was dreamed up by Christian Jank, a theatre set designer. He got his ideas for its "out of this world" appearance from the German castles of the Middle Ages. Some of the rooms were decorated with scenes from Wagner's operas. Ludwig's bedroom had a moon painted on the ceiling. (He slept during the day and wanted to make his daytime sleep time look like night-time!)

I NEVER KNOW WHETHER TO BRING HIM HIS BREAKFAST, LUNCH OR TEA

Unfortunately, all the money Ludwig spent on his mind-boggling buildings belonged to the public – they thought Ludwig and his ideas were completely mad. Ludwig lived in Neuschwanstein Castle for six months and was then sent to live in another German castle – a lunatic asylum called the Schloss Berg.

Himeji – the original "bouncy castle"

Himeji Castle, the Japanese fortress begun in the 14th century and more or less completed by 1609, really was designed to "bounce". Small earthquakes, or earth tremors, are common in Japan, so the castle needed protection. The builders had a mind-bogglingly brilliant idea: they made a base for the castle. The castle was built on top of the stones.

When there was a tremor, the stones wobbled, but the building stayed put!

SHAKING CASTLE

THE STONES MOVE BUT THE CASTLE STAYS UPRIGHT!

SHAKING GROUND

SHAKING ARCHITECT →

Himeji Castle never did fall down and never actually came under serious attack (although quite a few warlords did ask if they could visit and play on it for the afternoon). Even if it had been besieged it probably wouldn't have been damaged. Japanese Samurai warriors preferred to starve out their enemies, rather than attack them. One Japanese warlord even had dancers and musicians to entertain his troops as they waited outside a besieged fortress.

...AND FOR KENZO WITH HIS AMAZING DANCING GOLDFISH... ...NIL POINTS!

Last brick

It would be nice to think that the Japanese didn't destroy fortresses because they thought the buildings were so brilliant. But plenty of fortresses in Europe did get blasted to bits. It seems a pity that all that's left of many castles is a few nobbly bits in the corner of a field. But then, you might say that being bashed to bits was exactly what these castles were built for!

MIND-BOGGLING BOTCH-UPS & DISASTROUS DOWNFALLS

Have you ever tried building a mini skyscraper from a pack of playing cards only to have the whole thing collapse in ruins when a passing car backfires? All sorts of things can go wrong with real buildings, too...

- you can choose the wrong place to build
- you can choose the wrong sort of materials to build with
- natural disasters can come along when you're least expecting them
- the work can take much longer to complete and cost far more than you ever dreamed it would
- you can end up employing the wrong kind of builders – ones who aren't very good

...and you can end up with a building that's full of flaws...

Faulty tower

The secret of successful building is planning and thinking ahead before you begin a job. One of the first things you must do is to check out the ground you're going to build on and make sure it's going to provide a strong support for your building. No doubt the builders of the Leaning Tower of Pisa were wishing they'd investigated their foundations rather more thoroughly when they discovered, after only three storeys had been built, that the tower was tilting rather alarmingly.

116

Some straight facts about the Leaning Tower of Pisa

- The lean happened because the tower's foundations are set in soft, moist ground.
- The tower – which is 13 storeys and 54 m (175 ft) high – was begun in 1173 and completed in 1350. It houses the bell used to call people to worship at the cathedral next door.
- The tower is now 5 m (16 ft) "out of true" – in other words, if you dropped a custard tart in a direct vertical line from the top it would land five metres from the edge of the base.
- The famous Italian mathematician and astronomer, Galileo (1546–1642), used the tower to drop different-sized metal balls from, so that he could prove his theory

SORRY! I WAS JUST TESTING OUT A MATHEMATICAL THEORY!

about things falling at the same speed despite their weight.

- The tower has been leaning about one millimetre ($^1/_{32}$ in) further each year – in recent years this rate of "lean" has increased drastically.
- There are 294 steps leading to the top – as you walk up them you can feel the pull of gravity. Don't worry, though, you won't have to climb it – it's now closed to visitors for safety reasons!

Since the tower was completed, architects, engineers and builders have all been bending over backwards to put it back on the (almost) straight and narrow. The tower attracts thousands of tourists to Pisa every year so no one wants it completely straight, but on the other hand they don't want it to fall over either – somehow, the idea of taking a trip to see the Completely Horizontal Tower of Pisa doesn't sound quite as exciting, does it?

How *do* you prevent the tower from toppling while keeping that tantalizing tilt? Some of these ideas have been tried or suggested – and some are just made up. Which are which?

1 Hang hundreds of tonnes of lead from the tower to make it lean the other way. TRUE/FALSE

I FEEL DIZZY!

2 Issue visitors with special spectacles which make the tower *appear* to be perfectly vertical. TRUE/FALSE

3 Bury a huge refrigerator beneath the tower so that the

soft ground it's built on is permanently frozen solid.
TRUE/FALSE

4 Employ a local tug-of-war team to haul on a rope attached to the top of the tower while a gang of labourers shovel soil into the gap as fast as they possibly can. TRUE/FALSE

5 Drill holes in the ground under the tower so that it settles back into place. TRUE/FALSE

6 Build an identical leaning tower next to it so that the two buildings eventually touch and form the "Symmetrical Arch of Pisa". TRUE/FALSE

7 Surround the tower with a metal cage to stop it leaning further (sort of a walking frame for old buildings). TRUE/FALSE

8 Plant electrodes (electrical conductors) beneath the tower to take the moisture from the soil. TRUE/FALSE

A fissure ... a fissure ... all fall down!

At least the Leaning Tower of Pisa wasn't built on a geological fault – that's a sort of enormous crack (or fissure) in the Earth's crust.

The whole of the American city of San Francisco is built on a 1,760-km (800-mile) long fissure, which geologists have named the San Andreas Fault.

In 1906, San Francisco was only 60 years old and it was already world famous for its magnificent buildings and its beautiful bayside setting – many people described it as the "American Paris". On 18 April the plates of the Earth's crust alongside the San Andreas fault decided to throw a wobbly – in other words there was an earthquake...

- Eyewitnesses described a "frightful roaring ... that seemed a quarter of an hour before it stopped" – in actual fact the whole tremor lasted only three minutes.
- A journalist who saw the earthquake happen said...

BIG BUILDINGS WERE CRUMBLING AS ONE MIGHT CRUSH A BISCUIT IN ONE'S HAND

- More than 28,000 buildings were destroyed by the earthquake and the huge fire that followed – including 29 complete schools!
- Ninety per cent of the buildings in San Francisco were made from wood or wood sheathed in brick – perfect material for the fire that went on to engulf so much of the city.
- Co-ordinating the operation to save the buildings was the job of the Chief of the Fire Brigade. He was unable to help though – he was already dead! Having been wakened by the first violent tremors of the earthquake and the sound of falling buildings he'd leapt from his bed, dashed out of his bedroom door and plunged to his death as he stepped into the space where his landing and stairs had stood just moments earlier.
- The buildings that survived the earthquake were steel-framed (like modern skyscrapers). Since then people living on geological faults have tended to use this building technique. Some buildings in earthquake-prone areas have even

been built on special rubber foundations – so that they just bounce up and down during a tremor, rather than falling over!

How getting a big building wrong can lead to a "big bill" ding-dong!

The builders of San Francisco were no doubt kept extremely busy working out estimates for repairs and rebuilding work immediately after that terrible earthquake. It's always difficult to estimate the cost of a building before you start work. You can never be too sure what problems you're going to come across. The original *estimate* for the famous Sydney Opera House was *£5 million*, but the final bill was nearer *£90 million*. This is what happened...

The story of The Sydney Opera House – a comic opera in several phases

Early 1950s Good news – young Danish architect, Jorn Utzon, gazes wistfully at Bojnork Castle, Elsinore, Denmark (where Shakespeare's *Hamlet* is set) and gets an urge to design a great building.

1955 Even better news – Australians launch a competition for the best architect's plan for a new opera house to be built at Bennelong Point, on Sydney harbour. Jorn collaborates on a design for a building in the shape of five great shells or billowing sails, and wins! Whoopee! Jorn describes his design as "a symphony".

1959 Bad news – work commences on the Opera House, but Jorn's original design turns out to be unbuildable! The 60-m (200-ft) high shells which he thought would be self-supporting will need to be held up by sturdy arches – so at 26,000 tonnes (give or take the odd seagull or two), the roof becomes the heaviest in the world. Costs (and temperatures) begin to rise!

Early 1960s More bad news – all sorts of crazy building problems slow progress and add to bills – for example walls are built, then knocked down, because they're in the way of workmen who want to move their machines from one part of the building to another! The Australian Minister of Works now *also* describes the Opera House as a symphony – an unfinished symphony!

1966 Good news – most of the work on the main structure is finished.

Bad news – Jorn's long standing ding-dong with Australian government over soaring building costs comes to a head … Jorn has big sulk … leaves Australia. No finished Opera House! No architect!

Good news – team of Australian architects take over. Good on yer, cobbers!

Bad news – due to problems with increasing costs and lots more tiffs and wranglings it's decided that operas will take place in one of the smaller halls in the building, while others will be used for cinemas, TV broadcasts, etc. Perhaps it should be renamed the Sydney *Soap* Opera House?

1970s Good news – official opening day draws near – excitement mounts!

Bad news – someone realizes they've forgotten to build any car parks! And it's too late to fit them in. Oops!

Good news – someone has the idea of building *underground* car parking area beneath a nearby public park. Brilliant – better get busy!

Bad news – building workers refuse to fell sacred trees growing in park – it is a historic and special Aboriginal site.

Good news – opening night is almost here. Invitations are sent out!

Bad news – The Sydney Symphony Orchestra threaten not to play – they've nowhere to park their cars and the last thing they want to do is to lug their instruments through the city streets in their evening togs. Also, there are 75 musicians – but the orchestra pit is only built for 60. Help.

Everyone complains about backstage facilities – especially the toilets. They either don't work or collapse when people sit on them.

Good news – lots of frenzied last-minute activity saves the day – repairs to toilets are done and everything is sorted (more or less). So headline in local paper says: "It's all cisterns go!" (Well, they would … wouldn't they!)

Good news – opening night performance takes place. Everyone dead impressed – Opera House described as Eighth Wonder of World … Phew!

So that's that then – all's well that ends well – well, not quite...

1990s Bad news – new faults with the Opera House design are appearing all the time. It is estimated that by the year 2000, repair costs could run into millions!

(PS Better make that *billions* – just to be on the safe side!)

Absolutely pre-fabulous

After a disaster like an earthquake or a war some sort of cheap and easy-to-build shelter has to be provided for people who've been made homeless. During the Second World War – when thousands of British people lost their homes – the government came up with the idea of housing them in the single storey, flat-roofed buildings known as "prefabs".

Fab facts about the flat-pack shack

1 It was possible to put up the houses in just one day. They were called "prefabs" which is short for pre-fabricated. This means that the house has already been made in a factory but it needs putting together on the building site. It's the same sort of idea as the flat-pack kitchen cupboards your parents have so much difficulty with.

2 Prefabs had about 2,000 parts and cost about £1,300 each. The main pieces were made from corrugated sheets – made from a mixture of asbestos and cement – which

were then bolted to a steel and timber frame on site.

3 Some of the metal for the prefabs' steel frames came from recycled Second World War army lorry parts. They were sometimes erected by German and Italian prisoners of war.

4 One of the main problems with prefabs was mildew, which was caused by damp and condensation – people's clothes went green very quickly.

5 In some places like Twickenham, London, prefabs were built so close to each other that you didn't have to go round to the neighbours for a chat and a cuppa – you just opened the windows!

6 Prefabs were designed in America and many of them came fitted out with a cooker, cupboards and a fridge – which in the 1940s was a rare luxury – the prefab sort even had the newfangled ice-lolly moulds in them, which must have been very exciting in those times of shortages and rationed sweets.

Last word
In 1946, a Mrs Parker said of her new prefab...

It's grand. I would be prepared to live in it for the rest of my life.

She probably did! Despite the fact that the prefabs were originally intended as temporary accommodation – over 50 years later some of them are *still* standing and *still* lived in.

Architecture spotting!

Keep your eyes peeled for "prefabs" – you may spot them in the suburbs of big cities – they're usually recognizable by their flat roofs and concrete walls.

Disasters waiting to happen

If you want to get a mortgage, or loan, to buy a property, you usually have to get the property insured, too. A buildings' surveyor comes to look at the property to see whether or not it's likely to fall down. No sensible building inspector could possibly have given the thumbs up to these three properties…

1 The Tower of Lincoln Cathedral, Lincoln, England

The Tower of Lincoln Cathedral was a disaster waiting to happen – either because a medieval cowboy builder had thrown it together in a couple of wet Wednesday afternoons or because a horde of hungry woodworm were munching their way through its timbers. During a service in 1293, stormy weather brought the tower crashing down on to the cathedral's congregation, killing three people and injuring many more.

128

A prayer is now said at Lincoln Cathedral which contains the line, "Deare lord, support our roof this night, that it might in no wise fall upon us and styfle (suffocate) us, Amen". (But, contrary to popular opinion, this *doesn't* entitle them to a ten per cent discount on their buildings insurance.)

2 The first Eddystone Lighthouse

This was the first-ever lighthouse to actually be built out at sea rather than on the land next to it. It was made from wood between 1696 and 1699 and designed by Harry Winstanley. Harry's greatest wish was to be inside his creation "during the greatest storm that ever was". His wish was granted just a few years later – the lighthouse and Harry were swept away during a massive storm in 1703.

The builders of the second Eddystone Lighthouse learned a lesson from this disaster and decided that the number two version would have to be much sturdier...

They were determined that the wind and rain weren't going to get this one! And they didn't!

WHAT D'YOU MEAN YOU THOUGHT A BIGGER BLAZE MIGHT CHEER UP THE SAILORS

3 The Holbeck Hall Hotel, Scarborough, England

This luxurious hotel was built on a clifftop overlooking the English Channel during the 19th century. In 1993 guests began to notice the little telltale signs that the hotel was perhaps not up to its four-star rating in the *Good Hotel Guide*...

- doors began to jam
- walls began to crack
- the front garden fell into the sea.

The more perceptive visitors quickly realized that something was wrong. It was – the hotel was about to get an extra bed – the seabed!

A few days later it was hanging precariously from the clifftop 50 m (150 ft) above the sea – and not long afterwards, as the waves continued to batter at the base of the cliffs, the whole of one wing tumbled into the English Channel.

I'M JUST OFF FOR A QUICK DIP!

Surveyor's recommendation – don't build too close to Europe's fastest eroding coastline!

How to get lost in a good building

Do you remember your first day at school – when the whole building seemed strange and unfamiliar, and a search party had to be sent out to rescue you after you got lost on your first trip to the loo? It's not just children who get lost in buildings – it happens to adults as well, especially if the buildings in question are as big and complicated as the new British Library which has been built in London to re-house Britain's vast national book collection.

On 2 November 1996, the first books arrived at the Library and all sorts of important people were invited to witness this historic occasion. It was reported that afterwards, as the guests were leaving the building, one of them, Mr Colin St John Wilson, looked a bit lost and seemed uncertain of the best way out. Luckily, a member of the library staff dashed over and showed him how to leave the building. Who was Colin St John Wilson?

a) the famous author whose book *Last Exit From Bookbin* was the first-ever volume to be placed on the library's shelves?

b) a well-known explorer and pathfinder who'd had one of the reading rooms named after him?

c) the architect who had designed the whole building in the first place?

Answer: Believe it or not, the answer is c)!

...THEN A LEFT, A RIGHT, A LEFT AGAIN, UP THE STAIRS, ANOTHER RIGHT, PAST THE DOOR ON YOUR LEFT...

Lost architects aren't the only problem associated with the New British Library ... for a start the whole building is just a *bit* overdue...

Reminder
From The Head Librarian
To The Builders and Architects, New British Library

Dear Sir/Madam,
We would like to draw your attention to the following matters, which are giving us cause for concern...

1 Your library is now **nine years** overdue.

2 After carrying out a general check of the building, officials have found a total of

---

230,000 faults (and that's not counting the spelling mistakes in the books!).

3 There are so many building errors to be sorted out that a new computer system has had to be purchased just to keep track of them all – and that alone has cost £49,000!

4 The library isn't big enough – it *only* has enough room for 11 million books – but there are **18 million** needing shelf space.

5 In order to keep up with the vast amount of new books which are published every year, you are going to have to build half a metre of extra shelf space, every working hour, for ever more. So get cracking!

6 The so called super duper "high-tech" electronically operated mobile bookshelves that are supposed to help us locate books swiftly and efficiently have gone bananas ... instead of sorting them for us, they've begun throwing them all around the Library!

7 To make matters worse, your building activities seem to have disturbed a local ghost. The spectre of a weeping man dressed in 18th-century costume has been reported wandering around the building.

I look forward to receiving your completed building at the earliest possible convenience! Yours impatiently,

Shhh'eila. B. Silent – Chief Librarian.

As if all the technical problems weren't bad enough on their own, some very prominent people have also criticized the way the library looks. Labour MP, Gerald Kaufmann, has described the library as...

One of the ugliest buildings in the world.

And Prince Charles – who actually laid the foundation stone for the library building – isn't very impressed either. He said that he thought that the main reading room of the library looked like...

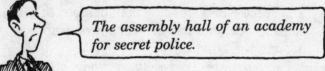

The assembly hall of an academy for secret police.

He also said...

It's awful ... it's just a dim collection of sheds groping for some symbolic significance!

Last brick

The British politician Winston Churchill (1874–1965) once said…

We shape our buildings, thereafter they shape us.

What he meant was, the look and feel of a building has a big effect on the people who live or work in it. The happier we feel about the appearance of the building we work in, live in, or walk past every day, the happier we'll be inside it.

TALL STOREYS

The sky's the limit!

Generally speaking, right from the damp and draughty days when staggering structures first got off the ground, buildings for living and working in never had more than six storeys. It was difficult to build tall buildings, because this is what usually happened...

Then, towards the end of the 19th century, buildings started to get taller. The big cities of the United States, like Chicago and New York, were becoming very congested and building land was getting incredibly expensive – so what better way could there be to save space and money than to build a skyscraper!

Three things made it possible to build them...

1 Architects had become better than ever at doing really hard sums. They could calculate how much each extra storey could safely weigh before the whole building staggered, wobbled and flopped to the ground.

2 A new building technique – which was learned from the bridge builders and engineers of the early 19th century – was developed.

3 People didn't want to walk up more than five or six flights of stairs. Although various sorts of lift had been used even in the days of the Colosseum, they weren't really reliable enough.

Then, in 1853, an engineer called Elisha Otis invented a safe lift. In order to get people to buy his invention Elisha had to show that he had absolute confidence in it, so he began giving spectacular public demonstrations to prove just how reliable it was...

- He had himself hauled up in the lift along with some heavy objects. And then...
- ...he got his helper to cut the rope supporting the lift.

Much to the relief (or disappointment?) of hundreds of astonished spectators he didn't plunge to his doom, because the lift was held in place by an ingenious automatic locking system.

People quickly realized that Otis lifts wouldn't let them down. In 1857, Elisha's company built their first steam-powered lifts and then, in 1884, a six-storey shop on Broadway, New York was the first building to have one of his newfangled "elevators" installed. In 1887 the Otis company built their first electrically operated lifts and after that there was no looking back (or down). Sales of lifts shot up – so did lifts – and so did tall buildings.

Architecture spotting!

When you are out and about, keep your eyes peeled for big buildings that are in the early stages of construction – look out for the vast steel skeletons that are being covered with brickwork, concrete and glass. And don't forget to have a look at the manufacturer's name on the next lift you ride in – it could well be an Otis.

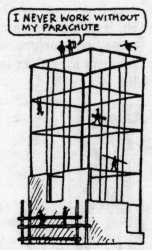

I NEVER WORK WITHOUT MY PARACHUTE

Iron ... but definitely not flat!

In the big cities of the USA sites for skyscrapers were few and far between, so if a piece of land became available for building, it was used, *even* if it was an odd shape! At the junction of Fifth Avenue and East 23rd Street in New York there was a bit of land that was just crying out to be developed. The

138

only problem was, it was triangular. That didn't stop the "do anything – sky's the limit" Chicago architect, Daniel Burnham, from finding a gold miner who'd just struck it rich in Colorado, then persuading him that it was the perfect spot to invest his new-found wealth.

The building was finished in 1902 and was the tallest building in America. It soon became known as the "Flat Iron" Building because its shape reminded people of those old-fashioned irons.

WHERE D'YOU WANT THIS BUILDING PLUGGED IN?

Over the top?

Not everyone was wowed by the new concrete, cloud-clobbering constructions. Some people thought they were all ugly and over the top. When an American pointed out a skyscraper to the visiting British Prime Minister, A.J. Balfour (1848–1930), and proudly told him that it was "fireproof", the British PM calmly replied...

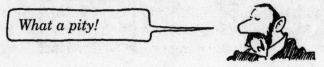

What a pity!

High, ho ... high, ho ... it's up to work we go!
It's New York, the 1920s – skyscraper mania is taking hold in America and two mega-powerful business tycoons are meeting with architects...

1 An architect called H. Craig Severance is commissioned to design the world's highest building for the Bank of Manhattan...

2 Meanwhile, Craig's rival and ex-business partner, architect William Van Alen is being commissioned by Walter T. Chrysler to create a posh new HQ for his car manufacturing company...

3 Work commences on the buildings...

140

4 As the skyscrapers near completion, it looks as though Craig's going to be top of the blocks...

5 William has secretly been constructing a 37 m (123 ft) stainless-steel spire – he is now ready to pull his master stroke...

6 At the last moment he "posts" the spire through the roof of the Chrysler Building – instantly making it taller than the bank building by 36 m (121 ft)...

Not only did William create a whopper that was a topper, he also made the skyscraper that nine out of ten tourists who visit New York still say is their favourite building. This may be because William paid so much attention to the all-important decorative details. As well as telling him to build a big building, Mr Chrysler had said that he wanted it to look just like one of his products. William based all the details of the 77-storey building on a 1929 Chrysler Plymouth car, just like this...

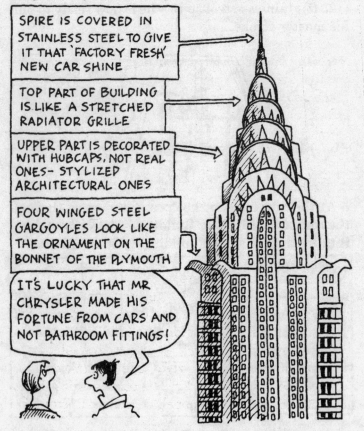

SPIRE IS COVERED IN STAINLESS STEEL TO GIVE IT THAT 'FACTORY FRESH' NEW CAR SHINE

TOP PART OF BUILDING IS LIKE A STRETCHED RADIATOR GRILLE

UPPER PART IS DECORATED WITH HUBCAPS, NOT REAL ONES— STYLIZED ARCHITECTURAL ONES

FOUR WINGED STEEL GARGOYLES LOOK LIKE THE ORNAMENT ON THE BONNET OF THE PLYMOUTH

IT'S LUCKY THAT MR CHRYSLER MADE HIS FORTUNE FROM CARS AND NOT BATHROOM FITTINGS!

The entrance hall is made from red marble, granite and chrome and has an enormous 29 m by 30 m (97 ft by 100 ft) ceiling painting showing stirring scenes of industry and transport in action.

The Chrysler Building was built and decorated inside and out in the streamlined "Art Deco" style that was popular in the 1920s and 30s – all sorts of things, from teapots to tram stops, were given the Art Deco treatment. The Chrysler Building was intended to be "of its time" – it still looks amazing!

Mind-boggling fact
In the high-flying world of skyscraper construction no one stays on top for long – just one year after they were completed, both the Bank of Manhattan Tower and the Chrysler Building were made to look quite titchy by this monster...

The Empire State Building

- The Empire State Building is situated at 350 Fifth Avenue, West 34th St, New York City, America. It is named after New York State and until 1972, it was the tallest building in the world.
- The main building is 380 m (1,250 ft) high and has a total of 102 storeys.
- It was built with 10 million bricks; 6,500 windows; 112 km (50 miles) of water pipes and 80 km (35 miles) of radiator pipe (and 5,000 pairs of those special builders' trousers that show the crack of their bottom when they bend down).
- And the rest – 7,600 km of electrical wire (that's 4,723 miles of it – enough to make an extension

cable that would stretch from London, England, to Beijing in China!); 61,000 tonnes of steel for the frame plus 5,600 cubic metres of limestone and 740 tonnes of aluminium and stainless steel for the outer walls.

● Construction work began in January 1930 and was completed on 11 April 1931.

● As many as 3,500 tradespeople worked day and night to complete the building – 14 of them were killed as a result of accidents that occurred during the construction.

● Many of the building workers were Mohawk Indians – they were chosen because they seemed to have no fear of heights.

- The builders built an average of four new storeys a *week*!
- The building was completed during the great American economic Depression. At first, only a few people could afford to rent office space, so it soon became known as "The *Empty* State Building".

- In 1945 a B52 bomber aeroplane crashed into the side of the 78th and 79th floors of the Empire State Building in thick fog – the aircraft crew and 12 office workers were killed but the building's main structure was saved from major damage by its strong steel frame.
- It was once hit by lightning nine times in 20 minutes.
- The powerful modern warning lights near the top of the building can be seen from 130 km (80 miles) away by people on the ground and from 490 km (300 miles) away by people in aeroplanes.
- The building is affected by high winds – on extra gusty days the observation platform at the top sways a distance of up to one metre (about three feet).
- There are 73 elevators in the Empire State Building, the quickest travels at 3 m (20 ft) in just one second!

- An Empire State "run-up" is held each year. Competitors race against each other to see who can be the first to climb the 1,860 steps to the top. It takes the fastest just 11 minutes to get to the 102nd floor. A normal person takes a whole half an hour just to come *down* the stairs (unless they decide to slide down the bannister).

- Some building experts are worried that the steel frame of the Empire State Building will eventually be affected by metal fatigue and sooner or later it will have to be demolished. If this did happen it would take 200 trucks working non-stop, night and day for six months to remove all the rubble.

- On 2 December 1979, a 29-year-old-woman called Elvita Adams climbed to the top of the Empire State Building then hurled herself into space – seconds later a freak gust of wind picked her up and blew her straight back on to the ledge she had just jumped from! The only injury she suffered was a broken hip.

Going one better

Of course, since the 1970s, the Empire State Building has been overtaken by all sorts of tall structures like the "breathtakingly ugly" (as one American writer described it) Sears Tower in Chicago which stands at 443 m (1,448 ft) and the whopping great CN Tower in Toronto which is over 553 m (1,800 ft) tall. It seems that there's no limit to the heights builders will aim for. So, how do you really outbuild the opposition? Well, you go "one better" of course – you double the rubble and build *twin* skyscrapers!

1 The World Trade Centre – New York

What's it like? It's got twin towers, 110 floors and it's a quarter of a mile high. Each tower has 99 lifts!

Crumbs! What's it all for? 50,000 people spend each working day inside it – having "meetings", tapping computer keyboards,

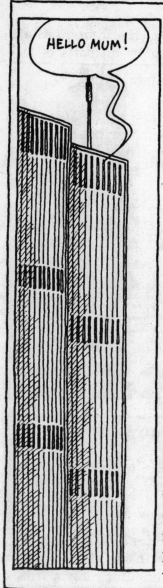

staring at screens, making business deals, sighing, yawning, that sort of thing! It also has 80,000 visitors each day.

So, you could say it's the biggest ants' nest in the world? Yup!

What's the quickest way to get up and down it? Well, as a visitor you will be permitted to use the "express elevator". That's the one that makes the ones in the Empire State look like sleepy snails – it goes from the ground to the 107th floor in 58 seconds flat (well, vertically actually!). A word of warning – don't try and get out while it's moving!

Worst moment? A terrorist bomb on the first floor injured 10,000 people. The walls ran red – not with blood, with wine. The explosion smashed $2,000,000 worth of plonk bottles to smithereens!

Three of the most hair-raising things visitors have got up to...

1974 Philippe Petit walked from one tower top to the other on a tightrope. He was arrested and as a punishment he was ordered to do free performances of tightrope walking for children in Central Park.

1975 Owen Quinn parachuted off the top.

1977 George Willig used crampons (spiked climbing shoes) of his own design to climb up one of the towers – he was sued for $250,000 – but only paid $1.10.

2 The Petronas Towers

Where are they? Kuala Lumpur, Malaysia.

Claim to fame? The tallest building in the world.

WOW! So, exactly how tall are they? 451.9 m (1,480 ft) – that's 88 storeys if you're counting.

What have people said about them? One man said that they're "impossibly romantic ... a poesy and drama that has an echo in everybody" (whatever that means).

He obviously liked them then! Definitely! He was the architect!

Anybody not like them? Ooh yes! One man said that they looked like "a huge cruet set" (salt and pepper containers) – then again, *he* was an "architecture critic".

What are they for? The Prime Minister of Malaysia says that they "symbolize and advertise the onward march of industrial growth".

So they're just a couple of really tall office blocks then? Yup!

WHERE DID ALL THE OTHER FLOORS GO ?

If you want to grab a slice of skyscraper action you'll have to be quick or someone's definitely going to beat you in the race to the top!

Develop your very own skyscraper!

Do you fancy making more dosh than you can shake a skyscraper-sized piggy bank at? Nothing could be simpler. All you have to do is put up a big building and rent out the office space to top international companies! Here's how to do it in 12 easy steps...

1 Get some help

ARCHITECT

I DESIGN THE BUILDING, EMPLOY LOTS OF OTHER PEOPLE TO WORK ON IT AND INSPECT THE WORK AS IT GOES ALONG...

BUILDING CONTRACTOR

I ORGANIZE THE ACTUAL BUILDING, EMPLOY THE SUB-CONTRACTORS, STEEL ERECTORS, ELECTRICIANS, PLUMBERS, PAINTERS AND LABOURERS...

QUANTITY SURVEYOR

I DO LOTS OF REALLY BIG SUMS, THEN TELL YOU HOW MUCH, MATERIAL, LABOUR, MONEY AND TIME YOU'LL NEED...

ELECTRICAL ENGINEER

I PLAN THE ESSENTIAL AND COMPLICATED ELECTRICAL SERVICES, WHICH PROVIDE POWER FOR LIGHTING AND COMPUTERS ETC

INTERIOR DESIGNER

I ADVISE YOU ON COLOUR SCHEMES, FURNITURE, FLOOR COVERINGS AND TOUCHES LIKE PICTURES AND POT PLANTS...

CHARTERED SURVEYOR

I PUT YOU IN TOUCH WITH PEOPLE WHO MIGHT WANT TO RENT SPACE IN YOUR BUILDING

2 Get a design

The skyscraper will be designed using CAD (Computer Aided Design), and a scale model is built – so that wind-stress tests can be carried out and the design can be shown to top business people who might rent office space.

3 Find a site

Position your skyscraper "strategically" so that it is a first-class place to do business from – make sure that it's...

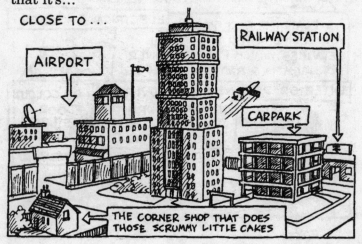

152

4 Clear your site

Got your site? Good! You must now call in a gang of rubble makers to get rid of any old buildings that are still on it – they will use a variety of techniques to do this...

5 Put in the foundations

A "geotechnical engineer" will check out the ground you are going to build on – if you're building where the ground is made up of soft clay you'll have to put in very strong, deep foundations.

6 Erect the steel skeleton

Before you go any further – a few words about safety! Your workers will be walking about at heights of over 400 m (1,200 ft) on metal girders that are perhaps no more than a metre wide so they are in great danger of losing things that are really important to them – like their car keys, breakfasts … and lives! Put up this poster on your site – now!

Danger!
Notice to all workers – especially those working at great heights

Don't play tag, leapfrog or five-a-side football during your lunch breaks.

Do wear hard hats at all times – a tiny bolt can do terrible damage to someone's head if it falls a distance of 30 or 40 storeys …

Do surround the structure with reinforced plastic sheets or nets to catch falling tools or other dangerous objects.

A NEW HAIR CUT

A HIGH SPEED CHEESE & PICKLE SANDWICH

A BIG MESS

Do attach yourselves to secure sections of the structure with a safety harness. Don't forget, at the dizzy heights you'll be working at you could easily be blown off the building by a sudden and unexpected gust of wind … so definitely avoid baked beans, pasta and cucumber sandwiches for the next few months.

7 Add the cladding

The steel frame's up – but something's missing! Well spotted – you still haven't put in the walls, floors or ceilings.

8 Put in your ducts

You are going to be putting in the "services" soon, like gas, electricity and water. Before you do this you must put in tunnels, known as "ducts", for the service pipes and wires to run along.

9 Add the waste disposal system

Your skyscraper is going to be a *prestige* building – the last thing you want is the occupants of the publishing company on the sixth floor lobbing the contents of their rubbish baskets out of the windows.

10 Make your building think for itself!

Add an extra computer system to turn your skyscraper into an "intelligent building" which will "monitor" (keep a check on) the services and warn occupants when there is a problem!

11 Put the finishing touches to your skyscraper

You're almost ready for the grand opening ceremony.

12 Give yourself a pat on the back

Your office space has been rented out to top companies – you're now a fully fledged property developer. You've overseen the project from start to finish – right from the day when you got local authority planning permission to erect your building. You *did* get planning permission, didn't you?

EPILOGUE

Buildings, buildings, buildings. They get *everywhere,* don't they? Sometimes it seems as if you only have to blink and another housing estate, out-of-town shopping centre or multi-storey car park has sprung up where only minutes before there were just fields, trees and cows.

If you're a keen architecture spotter, you will have noticed that an awful lot of buildings aren't particularly mind-boggling at all, and that others are distinctly dull. But this is what a couple of well-known architects reckon good buildings *should* be like...

Building ... plus delight.

Beautifully composed music crystallized in space.

Unfortunately, not everyone agreed with these architects' opinions. Sometimes it's a question of space, and sometimes it's a question of money – a nice Roman facade can cost a fortune, you know. Sometimes builders don't even ask an architect to get involved – it's cheaper not to bother.

But, why not see for yourself whether you think architecture's worth the effort? Check out some mind-boggling buildings in your area – from stately homes to skyscrapers, prefab houses to primary schools (yes, even school buildings can be interesting), there's bound to be something you can get excited about.

And if you're really interested, you might fancy getting in to architecture yourself. If you're brilliant at art and science, you could dream up some stunning structures of your own. You never know – they might even become the mind-boggling buildings of the future.

Also by Michael Cox...

Awful Art
In this imaginative guide, you'll meet rich artists, poor artists, dead artists and artists who made an exhibition of themselves. Find out about some forgers and fraudsters, and how to create your own priceless masterpiece. PLUS are you the owner of an artistic temperament?

Mind-blowing Music
Tune in to all sorts of cool musical happenings, from the birth of the blues to the amazing invention of a sound recording machine, and get into the groove with mind-blowing musical instruments. PLUS how to become an overnight pop sensation!

Smashin' Fashion
This go ahead guide will kit you out from tip to toe. Try on a hat that started a riot, slip on some pointy shoes that are three times longer than your feet, and meet the fashion designer who made rubber, zips and safety pins fashionable. PLUS design your own smashin' fashion collection!